C. H. SPURGEON
and the
METROPOLITAN TABERNACLE

Addresses and Testimonials, 1854–1879

"I would propose that the subject of the Ministry in this house, as long as this platform shall stand, and as long as this house shall be frequented by worshippers, shall be the person of Jesus Christ." These were the first words of Spurgeon at the Metropolitan Tabernacle.

Ernest LeVos

C. H. SPURGEON AND THE METROPOLITAN TABERNACLE ADDRESSES AND TESTIMONIALS, 1854–1879

iUniverse books may be ordered through booksellers or by contacting:

iUniverse
1663 Liberty Drive
Bloomington, IN 47403
www.iuniverse.com
1-800-Authors (1-800-288-4677)

ISBN: 978-1-4917-3403-2 (sc)
ISBN: 978-1-4917-3404-9 (e)

Library of Congress Control Number: 2014908179

Printed in the United States of America.

iUniverse rev. date: 10/14/2014

Contents

Preface

I would not have guessed, when I heard the name Charles [Haddon] Spurgeon for the first time in a Bible doctrines class in junior college in 1963, that a seed would be planted in my mind. In 2008, I would move from a devotional to an academic (research) interest in Spurgeon (and the Metropolitan Tabernacle).

It was in the 1980s that I read selections from Spurgeon, such as "The Unspeakable Gift", "Praise for the Gift of Gifts", and "God's Unspeakable Gift" – three sermons from the *Metropolitan Tabernacle Pulpit Series*.[1] Little did I know the value of his sermons for devotional reading, meditation, and research, but his genius of highlighting "The Gift" came alive when I possessed a copy of his popular devotional *Morning by Morning.*

Later, I purchased copies of both the morning and evening devotions, and beginning in 1988, I have read Spurgeon on a daily basis, especially his devotionals. I also read several of his sermons and books by him and about him.

My academic research interest in Spurgeon began in 2008 on a visit to London, when I learned of some original letters kept in the Metropolitan Tabernacle (a few more details of my research in London are included in the acknowledgement section with explanatory notes). I returned in 2009 to read these letters (I was informed that a handful of people had read these letters).

As a historian with an interest in cultural and intellectual history of the nineteenth and twentieth centuries, I am interested in sermon literature: what allusions and references ministers transport into their sermons from their environment and the society in which they live, and the sermons that they preach. This aside, it is my studied purpose to offer a documentary history of the ministry of Spurgeon and the Metropolitan Tabernacle from 1854 to 1879. It is about a working church, and Spurgeon believed wholeheartedly in a healthy balance between doctrine and practice. He viewed doctrine and practice as complementary and not contradictory. Selected addresses, sermons, and testimonies that best cover the twenty-five years of Spurgeon's pastorate and his working church are included in this publication.[2]

Prologue

Charles Haddon Spurgeon passed away on 31 January, 1892, but his "living faith" is inspiring. He is not the "Forgotten Spurgeon" 122 years after his death. He has been called the "Prince of Preachers", the "Heir of the Puritans", the "People's Preacher", the preacher who had "communion with Christ and his people", and one who lived "by revealed truth".[3]

> Spurgeon's first words at the Metropolitan Tabernacle were:

> I would propose that the subject of the Ministry in this house, as long as this platform shall stand, and as long as this house shall be frequented by worshippers, shall be the person of Jesus Christ. I am never ashamed to avow myself a Calvinist; I do not hesitate to take the name of Baptist; but if I am asked what is my creed, I reply, "It is Jesus Christ."

> My venerated predecessor, Dr. Gill, has left a *Body of Divinity*, admirable and excellent in its way; but the Body of Divinity to which I would pin and bind myself for ever, God helping me, is not his system, or any other

human treatise; *but Christ Jesus, who is the sum and substance of the Gospel, who is in Himself all theology, the incarnation of every precious truth, the all-glorious personal embodiment of the way, the truth, and the life.*

Spurgeon's last words at the Metropolitan Tabernacle were:

If you wear the livery of Christ, you will find Him so meek and lowly of heart that you will find rest unto your souls. He is the most magnanimous of captains. There never was his like among the choicest of princes. He is always to be found in the thickest part of the battle. When the wind blows cold, He always takes the bleak side of the hill. The heaviest end of the cross lies ever on His shoulders. If He bids us carry a burden, He carries it also. If there is anything that is gracious, generous, kind, and tender, yea lavish and superabundant in love, you always find it in Him. His service is life, peace, and joy. Oh, that you would enter on it at once! God help you to enlist under the banner of Jesus Christ.[4]

In 1879, C. H. Spurgeon celebrated his twenty-fifth year as pastor of the Metropolitan Tabernacle and his silver wedding anniversary. A *Memorial Volume* was published in 1879, and it included the sermons and addresses that commemorated the twenty-fifth year of his pastorate. Spurgeon himself wrote one short historical account of his ministry.[5]

This current publication incorporates primary source material from the Metropolitan Tabernacle *Minute Books of Church & Annual Church Meetings (MB)* 1854–82 (Volumes 1-6), from *The Sword and the Trowel (S&T)*, and from the *Memorial Volume (MV)*.[6] These materials and selections are included in Part I, "The Proposed Testimonial, Sermons, and Addresses", and in Part II, "Testimonial Meeting, History, and Presentation of the Testimonial".

Appendices are included. Appendix A covers Spurgeon's articles and two selections from the *MB*. These are the prayers of Charles Spurgeon and Pastor John Spurgeon, his father, on Tuesday, 16 August, 1859, in the ceremony of the laying of the first stone of the New Tabernacle and Spurgeon's comments at the meeting of the new church, the Metropolitan Tabernacle in Newington.

Appendix B has a testimonial to Thomas Olney at the opening of the Metropolitan Tabernacle in 1861, an account on "The Good Deacon" and a "Sketch of the Late Mr. Thomas Olney's Life" from *The Sword and the Trowel* by Spurgeon. The letter of condolences sent to the family of Thomas Olney (*MB*) is part of this appendix; it is followed by a testimonial to William Olney and his reply.

Finally, a list of the officers of the Metropolitan Tabernacle in 1879 is included. Spurgeon viewed and treated his deacons as more than good advisors; they were co-workers in the propagation of the Gospel. "For they that have used the office of a deacon well purchase to themselves a good degree, and great boldness in the faith which is in Christ Jesus" (1 Timothy 3:13). Thomas Olney, "a father to the minister", was a treasure to Charles Spurgeon, and so was William Olney, the senior deacon.

Acknowledgements
(with notes)

I would like to thank my university college for the professional and faculty developments funds I received from 2008–13 that enabled me, in 2008, to first attend the Seventeenth World History Association Conference (on "Global Cities, the Sea: Highway of Change") held in London. On a visit to the Metropolitan Tabernacle in 2008, Dr. Peter Masters, pastor of the Metropolitan Tabernacle since 1970, informed me of original letters of Spurgeon that I read on visits to the Metropolitan Tabernacle in 2009 and 2010, respectively.[7]

In the same visit in 2008, Chris Laws, an elder of the Metropolitan Tabernacle (Met Tab) and church organist, informed me of the annual School of Theology. Being interested in the integration of faith and learning (and life), I attended the School of Theology from 2009–14, and I am grateful for the many conversations I had with several of the delegates, laymen, pastors, and university students. Also in 2008, I purchased from the Met Tab bookstore, and read, John Flavel's *The Mystery of Providence,* which in turn led to a greater appreciation of Puritan preachers and their works.[8] As a historian, I acknowledge the role of providence in world history.

Besides, I researched and read several of the letters of William Wilberforce and the Clapham Sect (Hannah More, for one) in 2009 and

xiii

2010 in the British Library. In 2011, I pursued research on the Puritan views on the providence and sovereignty of God, Thomas Watson, and the Ejection of 1662 at Dr. William's Library (Center for Dissenting Studies). I also used the resources at the British Library, the Lambeth Palace Library (thanks to Dr. Masters for suggesting the library, with their collection from Sion College, and to Hugh Cahill, librarian, and his staff), and the Evangelical Library in London (thanks to the capable help of Steve Taylor, the librarian).

Besides, I am grateful for the use of the Heritage Room at Spurgeon's College in 2009 and 2010. Thanks to Bob Ross of Pilgrim Publications, Pasadena, Texas, for suggesting the heritage collection on Spurgeon and to Mrs. Judy Powles, librarian at Spurgeon's College, London.

I intended to continue my research on the Puritans, especially Thomas Watson. However, in July 2012, after being informed of the Metropolitan Tabernacle *Minute Books of Church & Annual Church Meetings (MB)* 1854–1882 (Volumes 1-6) and Surgeon's strong emphasis on a working church by Dr. Masters, I laid aside my research on Wilberforce and Watson. I spent a week reading the *Minute Books*, not wanting to pass up the opportunity to do additional primary source research.[9]

I continued my reading and the collection of additional content from the *Minute Books,* after attending the School of Theology, 2–4 July 2013, and added to and revised sections of this manuscript from July to September 2013.

Thanks to Dr. Peter Modern (Spurgeon's College) and Dr. David Bebbington (University of Stirling) for their encouragement and conversations at the 2012 Freedom and Power Conference, hosted by the Baptist Historical Society and held at Regent's Park College, Oxford, UK. Thanks also to Dr. Terence Crosby (with useful suggestions from his wife) in 2012 and 2013 on "how to handle Spurgeon".[10]

Special thanks goes to Bob Ross and his son, the late Mike Ross of Pilgrims Publications, with whom I had several conversations. With Mike I arranged to purchase several of Spurgeon's publications and especially the *Metropolitan Tabernacle Pulpit Series.*

I appreciated every conversation with Pastor Richard Rushing of Bethany Baptist Church in Martinez, California, and with Dr. E. S. Williams in London, UK. You were very encouraging.

Thanks to Dr. Joy Fehr, vice-president, Academic Administration of Canadian University College, for her interest and encouragement in professional and faculty development. Also, thanks goes to Kimhong Ung for word processing the material from the *Memorial Volume*, to Jillian LeVos-Carlson for her valuable help with Internet searches.

Special thanks go to the editors at iUniverse for their valuable help and suggestions.[11]

To the pastors, elders, deacons, members of the church staff, and several members of the Metropolitan Tabernacle (2008–14): I am especially grateful for your kindness and hospitality. "May the grace of our Lord Jesus Christ, the love of God our Heavenly Father and the Fellowship and Communion of the Holy Spirit, be with (you) and remain with (you) for evermore. Amen."

I wish to thank all who have encouraged and talked to me about my project, and I apologize to anyone I may have left out.

Part I:
The Proposed Testimonial, Sermons, and Addresses

1. The Proposed Testimonial to Pastor C. H. Spurgeon, August 1878 (*MB*)

For a quarter of a century the ministry of our honoured Pastor C. H. Spurgeon has been continued to his loving people with an ever increasing acceptance and power. Our church roll numbered at the commencement 313, and now 5346 person are known to be in our fellowship.

This fact demands a special "Memorial" and we therefore desire to show our gratitude to Almighty God by some mark of esteem and affection towards his honoured servant. For 25 years of faithful and eloquent teaching of Divine truth, no adequate return can ever be made, but we are constrained to attempt the expression of our feelings, in a way which we know will be in consonance with the wishes and judgment of our beloved Pastor, by gathering a Fund for helping him more easily to carry on some departments of that great life's work, which continues to grow under his hands.

We have resolved, therefore, to raise a sum of not less than £5000, as a thank-offering, for Mr. SPRUGEON at the close of the year; and the whole matter could be easily accomplished if every church member would give or collect £1.

It is our purpose to leave all donors at liberty to select which of Mr. SPURGEON'S many religious enterprises they would wish to aid with their gifts, but unless otherwise directed we think it best to unite in one special effort to raise a sum for the permanent relief and comfort of the many of the poor members of our church; as we know that our dear Pastor shares the spirit of his Master who said, "Inasmuch as ye have done it unto one of the least of these, ye have done it unto me."

In *The Metropolitan Tabernacle: its History and Work,* Mr. SPURGEON writes of the Almshouses connected with church, and of the heavy annual charge which the maintenance of our 17 aged sisters makes upon our Poor Fund: "We wish to leave the Tabernacle in good working order when our work is done; but the present burden might prove far too heavy for our successors, indeed, they ought not to be saddled with it. In future years the church may find itself barely able to support its own expenses, and we do not think that we are justified leaving it the legacy of so heavy a charge. Our present anxiety is to get the ship tight and trim, and this is one of the matters which is not in a satisfactory state, our aged sisters are worthy of all we can do for them and their grateful faces often make our hearts glad."

To remove this one care from our beloved Pastor's mind, and help a worthy object so dear to his heart, is a proposal we are sure will commend itself to all his friends. We therefore confidently expect a hearty response to our appeal to the many readers of Mr. SPURGEON'S sermons, and to all the members of his church and congregation to render this fitting tribute to him in celebration of his **Pastoral Silver Wedding**.

[All] Donations [are] to be sent to the Treasurers, T. H. Olney and Thomas Greenwood. Metropolitan Tabernacle, Newington. A **Bazaar** will be held at the close of the year, on behalf of the Almshouse Fund in connection with this Memorial. Contributions in money or goods will be thankfully received and should be addressed *The Secretary, Bazaar Committee, Metropolitan Tabernacle, Newington, and S.E.* Testimonial Committee, Metropolitan Tabernacle, Newington, August, 1878.

2. Meeting to Present the Testimonial, November 1878, Metropolitan Tabernacle, Newington (*MB*)

Dear Friend:

As the time for the presentation of the TESTIMONIAL to our dear pastor is fast approaching, we are anxious to ascertain the amount and character of the contributions towards it. We propose therefore holding a meeting of Mr. Spurgeon's personal friends on the 29th instant, in the LECTURE HALL, at 7 o'clock, for receiving contributions or promises on the accompanying form. We have asked Mr. C. H. Spurgeon to be present, and we hope to have an enthusiastic gathering. You will see that the whole value of such a tribute of love and esteem depends upon its being hearty and spontaneous, it is therefore of the highest importance that the proposed meeting should be numerously attended and warmly sustained. We trust you will make a point of being present, and of bringing with you any friend who will be inclined to aid us. It is so rare a thing to have a Minister spared to one congregation for twenty-five years, that any people ought to be stirred to commemorate the fact by presenting him with some token of their regard, but as we stand alone in the magnitude of the blessings received, we ought to be foremost in our recognition of the unparalleled goodness of our God. Our dear Pastor has been enriched with talents, influence and labours more highly than any Ministers we have known, and it becomes those who have profited by his ministry to show their appreciation of their privilege by cheerfully responding to such an invitation as this one. If you should be unable to attend the Meeting, will you please fill in the form on the other side and send it to the Treasurers before the 29th inst.

On behalf of the Committee,

T. H. Olney and T. Greenwood, Treasurers of the Fund

[Funds received as promised; directly or indirectly through the Bazaar £2,062.02]

3. "Twenty-five Years Ago: A Fragment" by C. H. Spurgeon, January 1878 (*S&T*)

Twenty-five Years ago we walked on a Sabbath morning, according to our wont, from Cambridge, to the village of Waterbeach, in order to occupy the pulpit of the little Baptist Chapel. It was a country road, and there were four or five honest miles of it, which we usually measured each Sunday foot by foot, unless we happened to be met by a certain little pony and cart which came half way, but could not by any possibility venture further because of the enormous expenses which would have been incurred by driving through the toll-gate at Milton. That winter's morning we were all aglow with our walk and ready for our pulpit exercises. Sitting down in the table-pew, a letter was passed to us bearing the postmark of London. It was an unusual missive, and was opened with curiosity. It contained an invitation to preach at New Park Street Chapel, Southwark, the pulpit of which had formerly been occupied by Dr. [John] Rippon, the very Dr. Rippon whose hymn-book was then before us upon the table, the great Dr. Rippon, out of whose Selection we were about to choose hymns for our worship. The late Dr. Rippon seemed to hover over us as an immeasurably great man, the glory of whose name covered New Park Street Chapel and pulpit with awe unspeakable. We quietly passed the letter across the table to the deacon who gave out the hymns, observing that there was some mistake, and that the letter must have been intended for a Mr. Spurgeon who preached somewhere down in Norfolk. He shook his head, and observed that he was afraid there was no mistake, as he always knew that his minister would be run away by some large church or other, but that he was a little surprised that the Londoners should have heard of him quite so soon, "Had it been Cottenham, or St Ives, or Huntingdon," said he, "I should not have wondered at all; but going to London is rather a great step from this little place." He shook his head very gravely; but the time was come for us to look out the hymns, and therefore the letter was put away, and, as far as we can remember, was for the day quite forgotten, even as a dead man out of mind.

On the following Monday an answer was sent to London, informing the deacon of the church at Park Street that he had fallen into an error in directing his letter to Waterbeach, for the Baptist minister of that village was very little more than nineteen years of age, and quite unqualified to occupy a London pulpit. In due time came another epistle, setting forth that the former letter had been written in perfect knowledge of the young preacher's age, and had been intended for him, and him alone. The request of the former letter was repeated and pressed, a date mentioned for the journey to London, and the place appointed at which the preacher would find lodging. That invitation was accepted and as the result thereof the boy preacher of the Fens took his post in London.

Twenty-five years ago, and yet it seems but yesterday, we lodged for the night at a boarding-house in Queen Square, Bloomsbury, to which the worthy deacon directed us. As we wore a huge black satin stock, and used a blue handkerchief with white spots, the young gentlemen of that boarding-house marvelled greatly at the youth from the country who had come up to preach in London, but who was evidently in the condition known as verdant green. They were mainly of the evangelical church persuasion, and seemed greatly tickled that the country lad should be a preacher. They did not propose to go and hear the youth, but they seemed to tacitly agree to *encourage* him after their own fashion, and we were encouraged accordingly. What tales were narrated of the great divines of the metropolis, and their congregations. One we remember had a thousand *city* men to hear him, another had his church filled with *thoughtful* people, such as could hardly be matched all over England, while a third had an immense audience, almost entirely composed of the *young men* of London, who were spell-bound by his eloquence. The study which these men underwent in composing their sermons, their herculean toils in keeping up their congregations, and the matchless oratory which they exhibited on all occasions, were duly rehearsed in our hearing, and when we were shown to bed in a cupboard over the dreams. Park Street hospitality never sent the young minister to that far-way hired room again, but assuredly the Saturday evening in a London boarding house was about the most depressing agency, which could have been brought to bear upon our spirit. On the narrow bed we tossed in solitary misery, and found no pity. Pitiless was the grind of the cabs in the street, pitiless the recollection of the young city clerks whose grim propriety had gazed upon our rusticity with such amusement, pitiless even the gas-lamps, which seemed to wink at us as they flickered amid the December darkness. We had no friend in all the city full of human beings, but we felt among strangers and foreigners, hoped to be helped through the scrape into which we had been brought, and to escape safely to the serene abodes of Cambridge and Waterbeach, which then seemed to be Eden itself.

Twenty-five years ago it was a clear, cold morning and we wended our way along Holborn Hill towards Blackfriars and certain tortuous lanes and alleys at the foot of Southwark Bridge. Wondering, praying, fearing, hoping, believing, we felt all alone and yet not alone. Expectant of divine help, and inwardly borne down by our sense of the need of it, we traversed a dreary wilderness of brick to find the spot where our message must be delivered. One word rose to our lip many times, we scarce know why, "He must need go through Samaria." The necessity of our Lord's journeying in a certain direction is no doubt repeated in his servants, and as our present journey was not of our seeking, and had been by no means pleasing so far as it had gone, the one thought of a "needs be" for it seemed to overtop every other. At sight of Park Street Chapel we felt for a moment amazed at our own temerity, for it seemed to our eyes to be a large, ornate, and imposing structure, suggesting an audience wealthy and critical, and far removed from the humble folk to whom our ministry had been sweetness and light. It was early, so there were no persons entering, and when the set time was fully come there were no signs to support the suggestion raised by the exterior of the building, and we felt that by God's help we were not yet out of our depth, and were not likely to be so small an audience. The Lord helped us very graciously; we had a happy Sabbath in pulpit, and spent the intervals with warm-hearted friends; and when at night we trudged back to the Queen Square narrow lodging were not alone, and we no longer looked on Londoners as flinty-hearted barbarians. Our tone was altered, we wanted no pity of anyone, we did not care a penny for the young gentlemen lodgers and their miraculous ministers, nor for the grind of the cabs, nor anything else under the sun. The lion had been looked at all round, and his majesty did not appear to be tenth as majestic as when we had only heard his roar miles away.

These are small matters, but they rise before us as we look over the twenty-five years' space which has intervened: they are the haze of that other shore between which rolls a quarter of a century of mercy. At the review we are lost in a rush of mingled feelings. "With my staff I crossed this Jordan, and now——." Our ill health at this moment scarcely permits us either to hold a pen or to dictate words to another; we must therefore leave till another season such utterances of gratitude as the fullness of our heart may permit us. Common blessing may find a tongue at any moment, but favours such as we have received of the Lord throughout this semi-jubilee are not to be acknowledged fitly with the tongues of men or of angels, unless a happy inspiration should bear the thankful one beyond himself.

The following items must, however, be recorded: they are but as a handful gleaned among the sheaves. To omit mention of them would be ingratitude against which stones might justly cry out.

A church has been maintained in order, vigour, and loving unity during all this period. Organised upon the freest basis, even to democracy, yet has there been seen among us a discipline and a compact oneness never excelled. Men and women associated by thousands, and each one imperfect, are not kept in perfect peace by human means; there is a mystic spirit moving among them which alone could have held them as the heart of one man. No schism, or heresy, has sprung up among us; division has been far from us; co-pastoring has engendered no rivalry, and the illness of the senior officer has led to no disorder. Hypocrites and temporary professors have gone out from us because they were not of us, but we are still one as at the first; perhaps more truly one than ever at any former instant of our history. One in hearty love to our redeeming Lord, to his glorious gospel, to the ordinances of his house and to one another as brethren in Christ. Shall not the God of peace receive our humble praises for this unspeakable boon?

That church has continued steadily to increase year by year. There have not been leaps of progress and then painful pauses of decline. On and on the host has marched, gathering recruits each month, filling up the gaps created by death or by removal, and steadily proceeding towards and beyond its maximum, which lies over the board of five thousand souls. One year may have been better than another, but not to any marked extent; there has been a level of richness in the harvest field, a joyful average in the crop. Unity of heart has been accompanied by uniformity of prosperity. Work has not been done in spurts, enterprises have not been commenced and abandoned; every advance has been maintained and has become the vantage ground for yet another aggression upon the enemy's territory. Faults there have been in abundance but the good Lord has not suffered to hinder progress or to prevent success. The Bridegroom has remained with us, and as yet the days of fasting have not been proclaimed, rather has the joy of the Lord been from day to day our strength.

The gospel of the grace of God has been continually preached from the first day until now—the same gospel, we trust accompanied with growing experience and appreciation and knowledge, but nor another gospel, nor even another form of the same gospel. From week to week the sermons have been issued from press, till the printed sermons now number 1450. These have been enjoyed a very remarkable circulation in our own country, and in the Colonies and America; and, besides being scattered to the ends of the earth wherever the English tongue is spoken, They have been translated into almost every language spoken by Christian people, and into some tongues of the heathen besides. What multitudes of conversions have come of these messengers of mercy eternity alone will disclose: we have heard enough to make our cup run over with unutterable delight. Shall not the God of the boundless goodness be extolled and adored for this? The reader cannot know as well as the preacher what this *printing* of sermons involves. This is a tax upon the brain of a most serious kind, and yet it has been endured and still the public read the sermons, best proof that all their freshness has not departed. Oh Lord all our fresh springs are in thee, else had our ministry long since been dried up at the fountain, the unction would have departed and the power would have fled. Unto the Eternal Spirit be infinite glory for his long forbearance and perpetual aid.

Nursed up at the sides of the church, supported by her liberality, fostered by her care, and watched over by her love, hundreds of young man have been trained for the ministry, and have gone forth everywhere preaching the word. Of these some few have fallen asleep, but the great majority still remain in the ministry at home and in the mission field, faithful to the things which they learned in their youth, and persevering in the proclamation of the same gospel which is dear to the mother church. When we think of the four hundred brethren preaching the gospel at this moment, of the many churches which they have formed, and of the meeting-houses they have built, we must magnify the name of the Lord who has wrought by so feeble an instrumentality.

Evangelists are now supported by the agency at the Tabernacle, and sent forth hither and thither to arouse the churches. Upon this effort a special blessing has rested, enough to fill all hearts with delighted thankfulness.

During a considerable period hundreds of orphans have been fed, and clothed and trained for time and eternity beneath the wings of the church of God, and many scores of these are now engaged in honorable business, prospering in life, in membership with Christian churches, and delighting to own themselves in a special manner children of the Tabernacle, sons of the Stockwell Orphanage. This is a well-spring of joy sufficient for a life. Those who have laboured with us in this holy work have a wealth of satisfaction in looking back upon the way wherein the Lord hath led us in this benevolent enterprise. Both the providence and the grace of God have been abundantly illustrated in this delightful service. If the story could ever be fully written—as it never can be—it would redound to praise of the faithful promise-keeping Saviour who said to us at the first, "My God shall supply all your need according to his riches in glory by Christ Jesus."

Nor is neither this all, nor can all been told. An army of colporteurs at this present moment covers our country; ninety or more men are going from house to house with the word of God and pure literature, endeavoring to enlighten the dark hamlets, and to reach the neglected individuals who pine alone upon their sick beds. Priestcraft is thus assailed by an agency which it little expected to encounter. Where a Nonconformist ministry could not be sustained for want of means, a testimony has been kept alive which has sufficed to fetch out the chosen of the Lord from amid the gloom of superstition, and lead the Lord's elect away from priests and sacraments to Christ and the one great sacrifice for sin. This work grows and must grow from year to year.

The poor but faithful ministers of our Lord have had some little comfort rendered to them by a quiet, unobtrusive work, which has supplied them with parcels of useful books: a work which is only ours, and yet most truly ours, because it is performed in constant pain and frequent anguish by her who is our best of earthly blessings. *The Book Fund* has a note all its own, but we could not refrain from hearing it as it swells the blessed harmony of service done during the twenty-five years. "She that tarried at home divided the spoil."

Time would fail us to rehearse the whole of the other enterprises, which have sprung up around us, and were we inclined to do so and to become a fool in glorying we should not be able, for bodily weakness pluck us by the sleeves and cries *"Forbear."* We will forbear, but not till we have exclaimed, "What hath God wrought!" Nor till we have noted with peculiar gratitude that to us is doubly fulfilled the promise, "Instead of the fathers shall be the children." Our sons have already begun to fulfill our lack of service, and will do so more and more if our infirmities increase.

It was right and seemly that at the close of this period of twenty-five years some testimonial should be offered to the pastor. The like has been worthily done in other cases, and brethren have accepted a sum of money which they well deserved, and which they have very properly laid aside as a provision for their families. In our case it did not seem to us at all fitting that the offering should come into our own purse; our conscience and heart revolted from the idea. We could without sin have accepted the gift for our own need, but it seemed not to be right. We have been so much more in the hands of God than most, so much less an agent and so much more an instrument, that we could not claim a grain of credit. Moreover, the dear and honored brethren and sisters in Christ who have surrounded us these many years have really themselves done the bulk of the work, and God forbid that we should monopolize honor which belongs to all the saints! Let the offering come by all means, but let it return to the source from whence it came. There are many poor in the church, far more than friends at the distance would imagine—many of the godly poor, "widows indeed," and partakers of the poverty of the poverty of Christ. To aid the church in its holy duty of remembering the poor, which is the neatest approach to remembering Christ himself, seemed to us to be highest use of money; the testimonial will, therefore, go to support the aged sisters in the Almshouses, and thus it will actually relieve the funds of the church which are appropriated to the weekly relief of the necessitous.

May the Lord Jesus accept this cup of cold water, which is offered in his name! We see the Lord's servants fetching for us, water from the well of Bethlehem which is within the gate, and as we see them cheerfully and generously setting it at our feet we thank them with tears in our eyes, but we feel that we must not drink thereof; it must be poured out before the Lord. So let it be. O Lord accept it!

4. "The Middle Passage"

A Sermon in commemoration of the completion of
the Twenty-fifth Year of his Ministry over the Church
meeting in the Tabernacle, May 18, 1879 (*MV*)

"O LORD, I have heard thy speech, and was afraid; O LORD revive thy work in the midst of the years, in the midst of the years make known; in wrath remember mercy" Habakkuk 3:2 (KJV).

HABAKKUK had the sadness of living at a time when true religion was in a very deplorable state. The nation had to a great extent departed from the living God; there was a godly party in the kingdom, but the ungodly and idolatrous faction was exceedingly strong. The Lord threatened judgment on the people on account of this and it was revealed to the prophet that an invasion by the Chaldeans was near at hand. The prophet, therefore, was filled with anxiety as to the future of his country because he saw its sinful condition and knew where it must end. The book of his prophecy begins with the earnest question of intercession, "O Lord, how long?" His spirit was stirred within him at the sin of the people and his heart was broken by a vision of the chastisement which the Lord had ordained. It becomes all who bear witness for God thus to be stirred in soul when they see the name of God dishonored and have reason to expect the visitations of his wrath. A man without bowels of compassion is not a man of God.

Yet Habakkuk was a man of strong faith, a happy circumstance indeed for him in evil times, for if faith be wanted in the fairest weather much more is it needed when the storm is gathering; and if the just must live by faith even when the morning begins to break, how much more must they do so when the shadows are deepening into night? Those who have tender hearts to weep over the sins of their fellows need also brave hearts to stay themselves upon God.

Habakkuk's name by interpretation is *the embracer*, and I may say of him truly that he was one who saw the promises afar off, and was persuaded of them and embraced them. He took fast hold upon the goodness of the Lord and rested there. In reading his prophecies one is struck by the way in which he realized the presence of God. Fitly does he entitle his book "the burden which Habakkuk the prophet did see," for in the vividness of his apprehension he is eminently a "seer."

He perceives the presence of God, and bids the earth keep silence before him. He beholds the divine ways in the history of the chosen people, and feels rottenness entering into his bones, and a trembling seizing him. God was very real to him, and the way of God was very conspicuous before his mental eye. Hence his faith was as vigorous as his reverence was deep.

It is in his prophecy that we read that wonderful gospel sentence upon which Paul preaches many sermons, "The just shall live by faith"; and it is in this prophecy too that we find that notable resolution of faith when under the worst conceivable circumstances she says or sings, "Although the fig tree shall not blossom, neither shall fruit be in the vines; the labour of the olive shall fail, and the fields shall yield no meat; the flock shall be cut off from the fold, and there shall be no herd in the stalls: Yet I will rejoice in the Lord, I will joy in the God of my salvation." Now, beloved, it will be well for us if we have much of Habakkuk's spirit, and are grounded and settled by a strong confidence in God; for if so, while we may have sombre views both as to the present and the future, we shall be freed from all despondency by casting ourselves upon him whose ways are everlasting. His goings forth of old were so grand and glorious that to doubt him is to slander him, and his nature is so unchangeable that to reckon upon the repetitions of his gracious deeds is but to do him the barest justice.

In the text which I have selected this morning with an eye to the celebration of the twenty-fifth year of our happy union as pastor and people, I see three points upon which I wish to dwell. The first is *the prophet's fear:* "O Lord, I have heard thy speech, and was afraid"; the second is *the prophet's prayer:* "O Lord, revive thy work in the midst of the years, in the midst of the years make known"; and the third is *the prophet's plea:* "in wrath remember mercy," coupled with the rest of the chapter in which he practically finds a plea for God's present working in the report of what he had done for Israel in the olden times.

I. First, then, I want you to notice THE PROPHET'S FEAR: "I have heard thy speech, and was afraid." It is the fear of solemn awe; it is not dread or terror, but reverence. Read it in connection with the twentieth verse of the preceding chapter: "But the Lord is in his holy temple: let all the earth keep silence before him. O Lord, I have heard thy speech, and was afraid." All else was hushed, and then amid the solemn silence he heard Jehovah's voice and trembled. It is not possible that mortal men should be thoroughly conscious of the divine presence without being filled with awe. I suppose that this feeling in unfallen Adam was less overwhelming because he had no sense of sin, but surely even to him it must have been a solemn thing to hear the Lord God walking in the garden in the cool of the day. Though filled with a childlike confidence, yet even innocent manhood must have shrunk to the ground before that majestic presence. Since the fall, whenever men have been favoured with any special revelation of God they have been deeply moved with fear. There was great truth in the spirit of the old tradition that no man could see God's face and live; for such a sense of nothingness is produced in the soul by consciousness of Deity that men so highly favored have found themselves unable to bear up under the load of blessing.

Isaiah cries, "Woe is me for I am undone; for mine eyes have seen the King, the Lord of hosts"; Daniel says, "There remained no strength in me"; Ezekiel declares, "When I saw it, I fell upon my face"; and John confesses, "When I saw him, I fell at his feet as dead." You remember how Job cried unto the Lord: "I have heard of thee by the hearing of the ear: but now mine eye seeth thee. Wherefore I abhor myself and repent in dust and ashes." Angels, who climb the ladder which Jacob saw, veil their faces when they look on God; and as for us who lie at the foot of that ladder, what can we do but say with the patriarch, "How dreadful is this place"? Albeit that it is the greatest of all blessings, yet is it an awful thing to be a favourite with God.

Blessed among women was the Virgin Mother, to whom the Lord manifested such high favor, but for this very reason to her it was foretold, "Yea, a sword shall pierce through thy own soul also." Blessed among men was he to whom God spoke as a friend, but it must needs be that a horror of great darkness should come upon him. It is not given to such frail creatures as we are to stand in the full blaze of Godhead, even though it be tempered by the mediation of Christ, without crying out with the prophet: "I was afraid." "Who would not fear thee, O King of nations?"

Habakkuk's awe of God was quickened by the "speech" which he had heard, "O Lord, I have heard thy speech," which is by some rendered "report," and referred to the gospel of which Isaiah saith, "Who hath believed our report?" But surely the meaning should rather be looked for in the context, and this would lead us to interpret the "report" as relating to what God had done for his ancient people, when he came from Teman, cleaving the earth with rivers, and threshing the heathen in anger. The prophet had been studying the history of Israel, and had seen the hand of God in every stage of that narrative, from the passage of the Red Sea and the Jordan on to the casting out of the heathen and the settlement of Israel in Canaan. He had heard the speech of God in the story of Israel in the silence of his soul; he had seen the deeds of the Lord as though newly enacted, and he was filled with awe and apprehension, for he saw that while God had a great favor to his people yet he was provoked by their sins, and though he passed by their transgressions many and many a time, yet still he did chasten them, and did not wink at their iniquities.

The prophet remembered how God had smitten Israel in the wilderness till the graves of lust covered many an acre of the desert; how he had smitten them in Canaan, where tyrant after tyrant subdued them and brought them very low. He recollected the terrible judgments which the Lord had sent one after another thick and threefold upon his guilty people, fulfilling that ancient word of his "You only have I known of all the nations of the earth, therefore I will punish you for your iniquities." He saw that burning text, "I the Lord thy God am a jealous God," written in letters of fire all along the history of Jehovah's connection with his elect people, and so he cried, "O Lord, I have heard thy speech, and was afraid."

Probably, however, Habakkuk alludes to another source of apprehension, namely, the silent speech of God within his prophetic bosom, where, unheard by men, there were intimations of coming vengeance which intimations he afterwards put into words and left on record in the first chapter of his book. The Chaldeans were coming up, a people fierce and strong, a bitter and hasty nation, terrible and dreadful. They were swifter than leopards and fiercer than evening wolves.

These were hastening towards Judah as mighty hunters hurry to the prey and in the spirit of prophecy Habakkuk saw the land parched beneath the hoofs of the invading horses; princes and kings led away into captivity; the garden of the Lord turned into a desolate wilderness and Lebanon, itself, shorn of its forests by the hand of violence. The fear of this frightful calamity made him tremble; as well it might, for Jeremiah himself scarcely found tears enough to bewail the Chaldean woe.

Now my Brethren, when the Lord leads his servants to look from their watchtowers and to guess the future by the past, we are also afraid. When we see God's chastisement of a sinful people in years gone by and are led to prognosticate the probable future of a sinful people in the *present* day, then do our hearts fail us for fear lest the Lord should avenge Himself upon the guilty nation in which we dwell. We are also afraid for ourselves with great fear, for we, also have sinned.

Thus, you see, the Prophet's fear was made up of these three things: first, a solemn awe inspired by the near presence of the Lord who cannot look upon iniquity, lest haply He should break forth upon the people as a consuming fire; secondly, an apprehension drawn from the past report of God's ways which He had made known to Moses and His acts to the children of Israel, lest He should again smite the erring nation; and then, thirdly, a further apprehension which projected itself into the future, that the Lord would execute the threatenings which He had so solemnly uttered by His prophets and permit the Chaldeans to treat His people as though they were so many fishes of the sea to be taken in their net and devoured.

Putting those three things together, I advance to the prophet's special subject of fear which has been generally overlooked but is very conspicuous in the text. The prophet was afraid because of the particular period of national life through which his people were passing. They had come, if I read his prayer correctly, to "the midst of the years," or the middle period of their history. Habakkuk's ministry was not exercised in the first ages when Moses and Samuel prophesied, nor yet in these latter days wherein we live, upon whom the ends of the earth have come. He probably ministered six hundred years before the coming of Christ, somewhere in the very center of human history, if that history is to make a week of thousands as to its years as many have imagined.

With regard to the Israelite people, they were now far removed from the day, "when Ephraim was a child." They were in their middle life when the best things ought to have been developed in them. The heroic age was gone and that unpoetical, matter of fact era was come in which men labored in the very fire and wearied themselves for very vanity and, therefore, like a tender intercessor, the prophet cries, "O Lord, revive Your work in the midst of the years, in the midst of the years make known." The application to *ourselves* which I want to make this morning is drawn from the fact that we, also, as a church, have reached "the midst of the years." Under the present pastorate we are like mariners in the mid ocean, distant twenty-five leagues, or rather *years*, from the place of our departure and making all sail for the further shore.

As to any service we may expect personally to render, we are certainly in the midst of the years if not near to their end. In the course of nature we could not expect that more than another twenty-five years of service could be compassed by us, nor are we so foolish as to reckon even upon that. We have at any rate come to middle life in our church relationship now that we celebrate our silver anniversary.

Brethren, there is about "the midst of the years" a certain special danger and this led the prophet, as it shall lead us at this time, to pray, "O Lord, revive your work in the midst of the years, in the midst of the years make known." Youth has its perils, but these are past; age has its infirmities, but these we have not yet reached; it is ours, then, to pray against the dangers which are present with us "in the midst of the years." The middle passage of life with us as individuals and with us as a church is crowded with peculiar perils.

Have you never noticed how previous dispensations have all passed away in their prime, long before they had grown gray with years? Upon the golden age of paradise and perfection the sun went down [before] it was yet noon. The patriarchal period saw a few of its hoary fathers wearing the veneration of centuries, but in a few generations men with lengthened lives had grown so skilled in sin that the Flood came and swept away the age before it had yet began to fade.

Then came the Jewish state with its judges and its kings and scarcely have we read that Solomon built a great house for the Lord before we perceive that Israel has gained the zenith of her glory, and her excellence declines. Even so was it in the Christian church of the first ages, so far as it was a visible organization. It began well, what hindered it? It was in full health and strength when it defied the lions and the flames and laughed emperors to scorn. But before long Constantine laid his royal hand upon it and the Church became sick of the king's evil, the cruelest of all diseases of the church of God. This malady, like a canker, ate into her very heart and defiled her soul so that what should have been a spiritual empire chastely wedded to the Lord Christ became the mistress of the kings of the earth.

Her Middle Ages were a night of darkness which even yet casts its dread shade across the nations. It seems as if the middle passage of communities cannot be safely passed except by a miracle of grace. The morning comes with a dawn of bright beams and sparkling dews, but before long the sun is hot and the fields are parched, or the sky is black with clouds and the glory of the day is marred. This is a matter of constant anxiety to the lover of his race who knows the jealousy of God and the frailty of His people, lest in the midst of the years the people should turn aside from their faithfulness and forget their first love, and, therefore, the Lord should be provoked to remove their candlestick and leave them to their own devices. O Lord, my God, grant this may not happen unto this, *thy* Church.

What, then, are the dangers of this middle passage? First, there is a certain spur and stimulus of novelty about religious movements which, in a few years, is worn out. I well recollect when we were called, "a nine days' wonder," and our critics prophesied that our work would speedily collapse. Such excitement had been before and had passed away, and this would be one among other bubbles of the hour. The nine days have lasted considerably long—may nine such days follow them in God's infinite mercy. Now, whatever detractors might say, we know that there was then a life, an energy, a freshness about everything which was done by us as a church which we could hardly expect to continue with us for all these years. Youthful novelty has certainly gone, and the danger is that a community should be greatly weakened by the ceasing of that force, which in some cases has been all the power possessed.

Lady Huntingdon, in a letter to Mr. Berridge, deplored the fact that every new work after a season seemed to grow lifeless, and Berridge remarks that in this the primitive churches were much like our own, and that after the former rain which falls at seed-time there is often a dry interval until the latter rain descends. I fear the good man's remark is sadly correct. From an admirable fervour many cool down to a dangerous chill. This is to be bemoaned where it has occurred, and it is to be feared where as yet it has not happened, for such is the natural tendency of things. Beloved brethren, I have prayed to God that when what is called the *esprit de corps* is gone from us the *Esprit de Dieu* may still abide with us: that when the spirit which grows out of our association with each other declines we may be sustained by the Spirit which unites us all to the Lord Jesus.

The middle passage becomes difficult, then, because things grow ordinary and common-place which aforetime were striking and remarkable. I do not know that this would matter much if it were not too often the case that with the stimulus of novelty certain other excitements vanish also. We tremble lest the people who prayed mightily at first should restrain prayer before the Lord; lest those who made many self-sacrifices should think that they have done enough and lest those who have consecrated themselves unto the Lord should imagine that they began upon too high a key and cannot keep up the music to such a pitch. A people who have loved the souls of men and have been like mighty hunters before the Lord after sinners, may suddenly dream that they are excused from further effort, and may leave others to do mission work for their Lord. It is an ill day when a feeling of satisfaction begins to creep over us, but this is one of the perils of "the midst of the years."

I have always been afraid lest that spirit of simple reliance in which we began should ever depart from us. It often happens in the commencement of religious movements that men are weak and few and feeble and despised, and they trust in God, and so they grow strong, but their strength becomes their overthrow. The tendency of our proud nature is to cease from childlike confidence in God when once it feels strong enough to rely upon itself. The Lord saveth not by many or by few, and if even for a moment we should glory in our numbers and think that now we are powerful for the achievement of any work which we may undertake we shall grieve the Spirit of God and He may in holy jealousy leave us to barrenness. This is to be dreaded beyond all things. My brethren, it is a glorious thing to be weak that we may have the strength of God resting on us; it is a glorious thing to be poor and mean, and despised, that the Lord may take such weak instruments and get unto himself glory by one use of them; but it is a grievous evil if in the mid-day of prosperity the church should vex the Spirit of God by self-confidence and cause him to withdraw his sacred succours.

Another danger arises out of the pride of achievement. When men are beginning to work for Christ they feel that they cannot do anything without him, and they trust in God to give them strength, and he answers their humble cry, and does great things by them. But when a good work is wrought we are apt to feel, "We have won our laurels. We have borne the burden and heat of the day, and we may now rest." This is fatal to progress. We shall do no more when we imagine that we have done enough. You know the story of the painter who broke his palette and put down his brush, and told his wife that he should never paint again, for the artistic faculty had departed from him. When she enquired how he was aware of the sad fact, he answered, "The last picture I produced realized my ideal and satisfied me and therefore I am certain that I have lost my power as a painter." It certainly is so, that we are fit for Christ's service so long as we feel that we have as yet done nothing, and are merely at the beginning of our purposed service. Those who pine for greater exploits have not yet spent themselves, but the danger lies in saying, "I have finished my day's work. Soul, take thine ease." From my heart I dread the middle hour of life's day, both for myself and you, for therein so many think it no ill, like the Italians, to take a *siesta*, or mid-day sleep, and then it is that the enemy is upon them.

There is, too, a pride of experience which is apt to grow upon churches and individuals, like moss upon old fruit trees, when men are "in the midst of the years." They feel, "we are not now the young simple, silly people that we once were, we are not now to be overcome by temptation or misled by error; we shall beyond all doubt remain sound in faith and pure in life even to the end." It is from the egg of carnal security that the canker-worm of backsliding is hatched; therefore we must mind what we are at "in the midst of the years."

Besides, I think, dear brethren, all Christians must be conscious that after a continuance in well doing we are apt to be assailed by weariness. Apart from our Lord's promised aid we faint, we die in the long race which he has set before us. Labour leads to lassitude and suffering to impatience. Grace is needed to prevent the decays of nature. When the natural spirits sink, we grow depressed and complain that our warfare is hard and our travail bitter; and with this there is apt to mingle a sense of disappointment, because we have not achieved all that our sanguine hopes expected. We scarcely rejoice that something has been done, because so much remains unaccomplished. When the mind is thus wearied the spirit faints at the prospect of a further and perhaps a heavier strain, and this makes the central regions of life wonderfully trying to Zion's pilgrims. We are apt to be slack in the service of God by reason of what we have already done, though that we must confess is little enough, Satan knows how to take advantage of our fainting moments, to make cowards of us if he can, therefore be ye aware of his devices.

If we have stood like watchmen on the walls for years the tendency is to relax our vigilance. If we have borne a protest for many years the thought will suggest itself that it will be folly to be singular any longer, and wise to yield to the current of the times. Then the enemy sneeringly whispers, "Who art thou, and what hast thou done with all thy testifying and separate walking and Puritanic precision? All that thou hast accomplished is insignificant enough. The world still lieth in the wicked one, and error is still rampant. Give up the battle, for thou canst not win." In the midst of the years, what with weariness and want of faith, the heart is apt to yield to the infernal suggestion; therefore, brethren, let a mighty prayer go up from the whole church to our Redeemer God, "O Lord, revive thy work in the midst of the years, in the midst of the years make known."

II. Thus have I indicated the prophet's fear, and now I would conduct you, secondly, to consider THE PROPHET'S PRAYER: "O Lord, revive thy work." His first request is for *revival*. He means, "Lord, put new life into us. Thy cause began with life, but the tendency of all around it is to make it die; therefore, Lord, quicken it anew, give it another birthday, and restore all the force and energy of its first love. Give a new Pentecost, we beseech thee; give all the spiritual endowments which came with the tongues of fire, and so enrich us anew. Revive us! Help us to begin again; start us anew in life. That is the petition, and it seems to me to be one of the wisest requests that ever fell even from prophetic lips. Let us use it. Lord, now that we have been twenty-five years together, let us feel as fresh as if the race were now beginning. Give us back the dew of our youth that we may do our first works, and something more. Let us have with the maturity of age the freshness of youth, and let us run without weariness in thy ways, because thy Spirit has quickened us. Our dependence is upon thee even for life itself; breathe thou on us once more.

And that life, as I understand it, is to come upon God's people themselves, "Revive *thy work*." What is God's work? Why it is God's people; for we are his workmanship. True revival must first come upon the churches themselves. In all churches there is much that is not God's work, and we do not ask to have it revived, but rather that it may be put away: but wherever there is anything that is God's work, any of the mind of Christ, any sincere prayer, any faith, any hope, any love, any consecration, we earnestly cry, "O Lord, revive thy work." Living saints alone are, in the exact sense of the word, capable of revival; we can only revive those in whom life is already found. O Lord, quicken thy people!

He means God's work in each one of us, for we each want revival; may the Lord send it to us now, so that if grey hairs are upon us here and there, and we know it not, we may become young again through his free Spirit. If the fountain of our life runs low may the Lord touch the secret springs and flood us again with holy zeal. To save us from the perils of "the midst of the years" we need to have life anew imparted to us.

But the prophet also refers to God's work *by* his people as well as in them. May the Lord put new life into his cause! It is an awful thing to see a dead church. I have seen such a thing with my own eyes. I recollect very well preaching in a chapel where the church had become exceedingly low and somehow the very building looked like a sepulchre, though crowded that one night by those who came to hear the preacher. The singers drawled out a dirge, while the members sat like mutes. I found it hard preaching; there was no go in the sermon, I seemed to be driving dead horses. After the sermon I saw two deacons, the pillars of the church, leaning against the posts of the vestry door in a listless attitude, and I said, "Are you the deacons of this church?" They informed me that they were the only deacons, and I remarked that I thought so. To myself I added that I understood, as I looked at *them*, several things which else would have been a riddle. Here was a dead church, comparable to the ship of the ancient mariner which was manned by the dead. Deacons, teachers, minister, people, all dead, and yet wearing the semblance of life.

> "The helmsman steered, the ship moved on,
> Yet never a breeze up blew;
> The mariners all 'gan work the ropes,
> Where they were wont to do.
> They raised their limbs like lifeless tools,
> We were a ghastly crew."

The Lord saves us from becoming such a ghastly crew. Now, to prevent our getting into that state, and we easily may, so that instead of devotion there shall be routine, instead of life and energy there shall be dead orthodoxy and dull propriety, we must cry, "O Lord, revive thy work in the midst of the years."

The prophet further asks for a fresh *revelation* of the Lord "In the midst of the years make known." When thou hast made us live then shall we have power to know, and therefore make the truth known unto us. Did he not intend by this petition that the Lord should make known that the work was his own? "Revive *thy* work; in the years make known," that men may not say, "this was only an excitement which the spirit of the people carried on for a few years," but may be forced to confess that this is the finger of God because it continues and abides. O Lord, in our case make the world know that it is thy work, because thou dost not forsake it. Again, convert multitudes, build up the church again, increase the people again, multiply the joy again, and pour out the Holy Spirit upon thy witnesses again with signs following.

But I think he chiefly means—make known *thyself.* In the midst of the years make known thyself, O Jehovah; reveal in the midst of thy church thy power to save. Make known the person and sacrifice of the Well-beloved in whom thy grace and vengeance strangely join. Make known the power of the Holy Ghost, who convinces of sin and afterwards comforts by leading the sinner to the cross. Make known thyself Eternal Father as thou dost receive prodigals into thy bosom and kiss them with the kiss of love, and make high festival concerning their return to thee. The prophet longed that God would be seen in the midst of his people, and this, above all things, is our hearts' desire. Oh, my brethren, it is vain and idle for us to think that any good can come of human speech or human song or human worship of any kind apart from God himself being there. There must be supernatural power put forth or men will never turn from darkness to light, nor rise from death to life. What is the church worth if the Lord be not known in the midst of her? You write Ichabod upon her walls, for the glory has departed when her God has gone.

The prophet virtually prays that God would do for his church again what he did for her in the olden time. We have just read the whole chapter, what a wonderful poem it is! We can only in a very prosaic way condense its meaning. First, with the prophet we exult in the manifestation of the divine glory. "His glory covered the heavens, and the earth was full of his praise, and his brightness was as the light; he had horns coming out of his hand." Thus was Jehovah seen, and our heart's prayer is "Lord, show thyself in this way again. Once more display thy glory. Stretch out that hand of thine which hath the horns of power going forth out of it. Exalt thyself in the conversion and the salvation of men that the multitude may see how glorious is the Lord our God."

Observe how the prophet speaks of God's power against his enemies. The Midianites came up upon Israel in such numbers that, like grasshoppers, they could not be counted; but the Lord smote them and utterly cut them off. Hear how the prophet describes their overthrow: "I saw the tents of Cushan in affliction: and the curtains of the land of Midian did tremble." And well they might when Jehovah came forth to smite them. Now our prayer is that the Lord would shine forth so gloriously in the midst of his church that the powers of superstition and skepticism may be made to tremble at his presence. I have looked upon their tents, wherein I have seen them multiplying their idols and their gods; I have looked upon their curtains, within which they have spoken proud words of carnal wisdom against the Most High, and my heart has said, "Let the Lord dwell in the midst of his people and manifest his power as in former ages, and these tents shall be in affliction and utterly pass away."

Moreover, the prophet sees all nature and providence subservient to God, and so he grandly sings, "Was the Lord displeased against the rivers? Was thy wrath against the sea that thou didst ride upon thine horses and thy chariots of salvation?" If God be with his people all things are on their side, the stars into the heavens fight for them, the wheels of everlasting providence full of eyes revolve with watchful wisdom, working out purposes of benediction. "All things work together for good to them that love God, to them who are the called according to his purpose." And all this he says was done for the saving of his people. Pharaoh and his horses were drowned in the sea, but as for Jehovah when he went to save his people, the seas could not overwhelm him; "Thou didst walk through the sea with tine horses, through the heap of great waters." Can you not see the horses and the chariot ploughing through the midst of the sea, while the Eternal King darts his arrows on either side that he may deliver his people? This is the language of imagery, but the facts surpass all poetry. God can be with a people, and he can leave them, but when he is with them their horn is exalted by his power and majesty, and the truth which they uphold is as a banner borne aloft to continuous victory. Only we must wait upon the Lord in prayer, and seek his face in faith, crying from our hearts, "O Lord, revive thy work in the midst of the years, in the midst of the years make known."

III. In the third place, let us consider THE PROPHET'S PLEA that it may be our own this morning.

He had first this plea: "Lord, it is *thy* work; therefore revive thy work." We take the words out of his mouth and pray in like manner, "Lord, if this is *our* work, end it; if it is man's work, break it down; but if it be *thy* work, revive it." Have we not said unto our souls that we will preach and we will believe nothing but what is revealed of God in the Scripture, but we will not yield one hair's breadth to the opposers of revelation, because of their so-called science and thought? Is it not even so? We have lifted the old banner of our fathers and preached the doctrines of the grace of God, whereof the very centre is Christ crucified a substitute for believing men. This has been our one theme, our staple subject in preaching and ministering at all times. Now, Lord, if this be not thy truth, for thy name's sake blight it, and let us follow it no more; but if it be thy truth, set thy seal to it here and in every other place where the name of Jesus is proclaimed. This is good pleading; "It is thy work. We cannot do it, we will not attempt to do it, but Lord, if it be thine, thou must do it, and we hold thee to it by humble faith."

But the best plea is the one he mentions, "In wrath remember *mercy*;" that is a plea which suits every one of us—mercy, mercy, mercy: Thou might test well smite both the shepherd and the sheep, but have mercy. Thou mightest well take away the candlestick and leave us in the darkness, but in wrath remember mercy! Thou seest the coldness of heart and the inconsistency of life of some of thy professed people, and thou mightest therefore give up thy Zion to desolation, but, Lord, remember mercy. Remember it, for thou knowest it; for mercy is a dear attribute of thine. Remember thy mercy in the everlasting covenant when thou didst choose thy people. Remember thy mercy in the seal of that covenant when thy only begotten Son was given up to death. Remember all the mercy thou hast had upon us these many years of our provocation; remember mercy and still favor us, not because we have any good thing in us or about us that can deserve thy love, but for thy mercy's sake. Out of thy free rich sovereign grace, for mercy's sake, still "revive thy work in the midst of the years." It is good pleading; be sure to use it.

One more plea is implied in the rest of the chapter, namely. "Thou hast wrought great wonders, O Lord; do this again in the midst of the years." Here hast thou heard our prayers; Lord, hear our prayers in the midst of the years; hear them now. Here hast thou helped the feeble against the strong; Lord, strengthen us yet again. Here hast thou brought the chief of sinners to Jesus' feet; Lord, do the like again! That is our prayer. By all thy glorious marchings though the wilderness when thou didst lead thy people and scatter their foes before them, when the rocks gave them water and the heavens dropped with bread; by all the wonders of thy grace to thy people of old, since they are still thy people, "revive thy work in the midst of the years."

With this I finish, observing that when the prophet had pleaded, and his soul was at rest, he sat him down, and there were three things which remained upon his mind. Peering into the future he saw the sheen of the Chaldean helmets and the brightness of their cruel swords. He saw the whole land turned into a wilderness, and as he watched he saw that the fig-trees did not blossom, the vines brought forth no fruit, the olives withered, lowing of cattle there was none, bleating of sheep was hushed, famine covered all the land and he said, "Lord, let it all come as I have seen, but thy ways are everlasting, and in the thick darkness thou hast always wrought thy will. Thou hast never been defeated, and thou hast never failed thy people; therefore, as for me I will rejoice in the Lord, I will joy in God of my salvation." That is the posture in which I want you all to be found. We have been assured by people who think they know a great deal about the future that awful times are coming. Be it so; it need not alarm us, for the Lord reigneth. Stay yourself on the Lord, my brother, and you can rejoice in his name. If the worst comes to the worst, our refuge is in God; if the heavens shall fall the God of heaven will stand; when God cannot take care of his people under heaven he will take them above the heavens, and there shall they dwell with him. Therefore, as far as you are concerned, rest; for you shall stand in your lot at the end of the days.

And then there came over Habakkuk a second spirit. Now, said he, seeing God hath wrought all these wonders of old, and is capable of doing them over again, I will go back to my work despite the lowering clouds, for "the Lord God is my strength, and he will make my feet like hinds' feet," like the gazelle's feet upon the crags of the mountains "and he will make me to walk upon mine high places." O for this assurance of safety and strength in the Lord! We are in the middle passage, but if we have faith in God all is safe. We may go and leap in our duties over the mountains and the hills, and not be afraid that our foot shall slip. We fall without our God, but with God our feet shall never slide. He keepeth the feet of his saints, and when the wicked shall be silent in darkness then shall the strength of the Lord be seen.

Having thus felt that he could always trust God whatever might happen, and that he should be upheld whatever might occur, what does Habakkuk say? He goes home about his business, and what is the one business he is set upon? He indicates it in his last sentence which is not a sentence at all, but the final words of his prayer, "To the chief singer on my stringed instruments." He seems to say, "All that remains for me is but to love and sing, and wait until the angels come to bear me to their King." "All that I have to do now," he seems to say, and I want you to say the same, "is just to feel that all is safe in the eternal hands."

As for me,
> "I'll praise him while he lends me breath,
> And when my voice is lost in death,
> Praise shall employ my nobler powers;
> My days of praise shall ne'er be past,
> While life, and thought, and being last,
> Or immortality endures."

5. "Crowning Blessings Ascribed To God"

The second Sermon in commemoration of the completion of Twenty-five years of his Ministry in the midst of the Church assembling in the Tabernacle, May 18, 1879 (*MV*)

"Thou crownest the year with thy goodness" Psalm 65:11 (KJV).

GODLY men in olden times felt God to be very near them, and they attributed everything they saw in nature to the direct operation of his hand. They were not accustomed to speak of "the laws of matter," and "the operation of natural forces," and "the outcome of divers causes"; but they thought more of the First Cause, the foundation and pillar of all existence, and they saw him at work on all sides. Hear how the Psalmist sings, "*Thou* makest the outgoings of the morning and evening to rejoice. *Thou* visitest the earth and waterest it. *Thou* preparest them corn when thou hast so provided for it. *Thou* waterest the ridges thereof abundantly; *Thou* settlest the furrows thereof: *Thou* makest if soft with showers; *Thou* blessest the springing thereof. *Thou* crownest the year with *thy* goodness." God was very near in those days. As Herbert says:

"One might have sought and found thee presently

At some fair oak, or bush, or cave, or well."

If the result of our philosophy has been to put God farther off from the consciousness of his creatures, God save us from such philosophy, and let us get back again into the simple state in which we were children at home, and God, our great Father, wrought all things for us. Let us note the distinct mention of God throughout the psalm, for it is well worthy of notice; and let our speech be more after the olden sort, with less of our supposed knowledge in it, and a good deal more concerning the presence and the goodness of God.

I am not about to use our text in reference to the outside world and to the husbandry of man, but we shall see how true it is within the church, which is the husbandry of God. The language was meant to describe the field of nature; but it is equally true of the garden of the church. I am going to use the text in this way, because of the peculiar circumstances under which we meet, celebrating, as we do, the twenty-fifth year of our happy union together as pastor and flock, a period which has to the fullest extent been crowned with the goodness of the Lord. If I use the text for spiritual purposes I shall not err, for there is always a most striking analogy between the world of grace and world of nature, so that it would be hard to find anything said by inspiration concerning the visible world which might not be correctly spoken with regard to the spiritual world.

But I do not depend upon that fact for my justification. I refer you to the psalm itself. It is clear that it was written to praise God, not alone for his works in the harvest-field and abroad upon the sea, but for his wonderful goodness towards his people, for thus the psalm begins: "Praise waiteth for thee, O God, *in Sion*." It is Zion's hymn which lies before us; and therefore the church which Zion represented may well appropriate the language and use it for herself, and say, concerning all the Lord's mercy to her, in her ploughing, her sowing, her watching, and the glad harvest of her spiritual husbandry, "Thou crownest the year with thy goodness." The spirit of the text is joyful gratitude, and my soul is so filled therewith that I do not want so much to preach to you as to lead you into holy adoration of God for the great mercies with which he has surrounded us as a church and congregation from the first day even until now.

I. And so our first head is DIVINE GOODNESS ADORED. "Thou crownest the year with thy goodness."

Whatever of acceptable service we have rendered, and whatever of real success we have achieved, has come from the Lord of hosts who has wrought all our works in us. Whatever of holy result may have followed from earnest effort, and whatever honour has redounded unto God there from is the Lord's doings, and it is marvelous in our eyes. "Not unto us, not unto us, O Lord, but unto thy name give glory, for thy mercy, and for thy truth's sake." Thy goodness, and not ours, has crowned the work; thy goodness, indeed, it is which makes every good work good, and gives to every good its crown. From its first conception even to its ultimate conclusion all virtue is of thee. From blade to full corn all the harvest is of thee, O Lord, and to thee let it be ascribed. Let us, therefore, praise the Lord with all our hearts for twenty-five years of prayer and effort, of planning and working, of believing and rejoicing, which he has crowned with his goodness.

We will try to follow the run of the psalm, and our first note shall be this: *praise must be for God alone*. "Praise waiteth for *thee*, O God, in Sion"; not for men, nor for priest, nor for pastors, presbyters, bishops, ministers, or whatsoever you choose to call them: "Praise waiteth for thee, O God, in Sion." Whosoever shall have done well in the midst of the church let him have the love of his brethren, but let all the praise be unto thee, O thou Most High. Far be it for the axe to exalt itself and forget him that felleth therewith, or for the sword to deprive the conqueror of his glory. Praise is silent while the best of men are passing by; it lays its finger on its lips till the Lord approaches, and then bursts forth in gladsome song because *He* appears.

Whatever else you do, my brethren, be sure that your soul magnifies the Lord and abhors the very idea of self-glorification. If the Lord has blessed you, shake off, as Paul shook off the viper from his hand, any idea of ascribing praise to yourself. We are mere vanity, and to us belong shame and confusion of face; these are, so to speak, our belongings, the only dowry our fathers have left to us. What are we that the Lord should bless us? Did you bring a soul to Christ the other day? Bless the Holy Spirit who helped you by His power to do so divine a deed. Did you bear bold testimony for the truth but yesterday? Bless Him who is the faithful and true witness that at His feet you learned how to be true, and by His Spirit were enabled to be brave. "Not unto us! Not unto us!" With vehemence we deprecate the idea of honouring ourselves. Again and again we put away the usurper's crown which Satan proffers us. How can we endure the base proposal? Shall we rob God of His glory? Even He from whom we derive our very existence? Perish, O pride, abhorred of God and man. O Lord, keep thou me from the approach of that shameful evil. Brother, if thou hast any esteem among men, cast thy crown at Jehovah's feet, and there let it lie. All honour is to God only.

In this spirit every action of the Christian church ought to be done, for what says the second clause of the psalm? "Unto thee shall the vow be performed." Brothers and sisters, we ought to praise God in all that we do, by doing it to His praise. There must be no motive of this kind; "I must give because others give. I must attend at such and such a meeting because otherwise I should be missed." Cast away from you, I pray you, the service of any master but your Lord in heaven, for two masters you cannot serve. Honour ye the Lord in all that ye do. Whether ye teach the classes of the school, or stand up at the corner of the street, or hand a tract to a passer-by, or preach to the multitude, let the vow be performed as unto the Lord. It is wonderful how sweet it is to do service when it is expressly done *to Him*. I do not marvel that the woman broke the alabaster box *over Him*. Breaking precious boxes, and spilling priceless nard, may be hard work of itself to selfish flesh and blood, but it becomes a self-gratifying luxury to do it *unto Him*. When all our life shall be doing service unto the Well-beloved, whom to serve is honour and delight, for whom to die were bliss unspeakable, then shall we have learned how to live. Lord, thou crownest the year with thy goodness, and therefore we would do all things as unto thee, expecting thy grace to assist our service, thy love to accept it, thy pity to forgive it, and thy power to make it effectual to thine own glory. Oh, that I had but power, and God the Holy Ghost has that power, first to take away from each of us all thought of self-glorification, and then to consecrate our entire being, even to our pulse and breath, to His praise whose love has make us what we are!

Further, brethren, in praising God, we may be helped to do so, and to see how he crowns the year with his goodness, when we *recollect our answered prayers as a church*. What saith the second verse? "O thou that hearest prayer, unto thee shall all flesh come." I say it and there is no boasting in the saying of it, but there is a glorying in God that prayers have been heard which have been put up by this church in ways and manners which have not been less than marvellous. Such of you as have been with us from the beginning will remember times when, in our weakness and in our poverty, we cried to the Lord for help, because of our need, and he heard us. Especially was this the case concerning the building of the house in which we are now assembled. Ah, how speedily he helped us. How liberally, how like a God! When we have needed means to feed the children of our Orphanage, the Prayer Meeting on Monday night has been followed by a response before the week has gone round. When two or three of us have met together, unknown to all the rest, to lay special siege to haven upon the appearance of troubles which we did not wish to tell to others, we have seen the arm of God made bare among us, and we could no more doubt it than we could doubt our own existence.

Oh, you that have had your prayers answered, praise ye the Lord who crowns your supplications with his acceptance. Remember that it is because of prayer that, as a church, we have continued to advance from strength to strength, and shall not our praises balance our prayers? If the Lord gives goodness, shall not we give gratitude? Our prayers confessed our dependence, we felt that our years could never be crowned unless the Lord crowned them, and, now that the blessing has come, let our praises prove our thankfulness while we cry, "Thou crownest the years with thy goodness."

And, beloved friends, it may greatly increase our praise of God for all his goodness *if we think of our many sins*. Have we tried to serve him? Alas, how often have we failed? The iniquities of our holy things might long ago have provoked the Lord to wrath. Among us has there not been much that his pure and holy eyes must have grieved over? The watchers of the church have sometimes come together in sore dismay over this and that which they have seen amongst the brotherhood, and they have cried to God that he would put away the evil thing from among us, or help us to overcome the evil one, and reclaim the wandering. Nobody knows but God all the cares and anxieties which surround those that watch over such a flock as this. Who is sufficient for these things? Have we been made sufficient? Then infinite grace has done the deed. The best of us, whoever they may be, will be the first to lie low before the Lord, and those among us who have exhibited a Christly character, and have served the cause of Christ heartily will the most deeply feel that if the Lord had taken the candlestick out of its place and left us in the darkness, we had well deserved it. Eternally blessed be the name of the Ever Merciful, when we have sinned we have always had an Advocate before the throne, and the blood of sprinkling has ever been upon us to make us clean in the sight of the Lord. Blessed be his name, though "iniquities prevail" against us, yet, as for our transgressions, he has purged them away, and still does his church lift up her face and live in the smile of his love rejoicing and triumphant. Beloved, this ought to make us praise God with all our hearts, and the psalmist manifested the wisdom of inspiration in reminding us of it.

And once more, *the sacred privileges which infinite mercy has bestowed upon us* should compel us with glad alacrity to magnify the name of God. See how the psalm proceeds. "Blessed is the man whom thou choosest, and causest to approach unto thee, that he may dwell in thy courts. We shall be satisfied with the goodness of thy house, even of thy holy temple." Many now present first learned in this house their election of God, for here they were called by almighty grace, and enabled to approach unto their heavenly Father. Blessed be the choosing and calling Lord who now gives us access to himself and nearness to his person. You recollect when first you drew near to him with weeping eyes and melting hearts, because his love had broken down your rebellious wills. Oh, it was a sorrowful coming, but it was a true coming, for God was calling you. And do you remember afterwards when you came to him with glad hearts and rejoicing eyes, for the Lord had put away your sin, and you stood "accepted in the Beloved"? Oh, that glad day! Last Sunday we sang:

"Happy day, happy day."

And we may sing it every day and every morning and evening of our lives and not sing it too often. The Lord who chose us and called us and made us to approach unto him has not since become our enemy, for he has allowed us ever since to dwell in his house. We are his children; we have not called upon him like strangers, but we have dwelt in his house as sons. He has been abiding with us, and we have been made to abide in him. Shall we not praise him for this? This very house of prayer has been to some of you a quiet resting-place. You have been more at home here than when you have been at home. I will be bound to say that you recollect more happy times that you have had here than anywhere else, and these have put out of your memory the sad records of your hard battling in the world, even for a livelihood.

I know that many of you live by your Sabbaths. You step over the intervening space from Lord's-day to Lord's-day, as if the Lord had made a ladder of Sabbaths for you to climb to heaven by. And you have been fed in the Lord's house as well as rested. I know you have, for he who deals out the meat has been fed himself, and when he is fed he knows that others have like appetites, and need like food, and know when they get it. You have clapped your hands for very joy when redeeming grace and dying love have been the theme, and infinite, sovereign, changeless mercy has been the subject of discourse. Well now, by every happy Sabbath you have had, my brethren; by every holy Monday evening's prayer meeting; by every occasion on which God has met with you in any of the rooms of this building, when a few of you at early morning or late in the evening have met together for prayer; by every time in which the visits of Jesus' love have charmed your soul up to heaven's gate, bless and magnify his name, who has crowned the years with his goodness. There had been no food for us if the Lord had not given us manna from heaven. There had been no comfortable rest for us if he had not breathed peace upon us. There had been no coming in of new converts, nor going out with rapturous joy of the perfected ones up to the seats above, if the Lord had not been with us, and therefore to him be all the praise.

I do not suppose that any stranger here will understand this matter. It may even be that such will judge that we are indulging in self-gratulation under a thin disguise; but this evil we must endure for once. You, my brothers and sisters, who have been together these many years, know what is meant, and you know that it is not within the compass of an angel's tongue to express the gratitude which many of us feel who for these five-twenty years have been banded together in closest and heartiest Christian brotherhood in the service of our Lord and Master.

Strangers cannot guess how happy has been our fellowship, or how true our love. Eternity alone shall reveal the multitude of mercies with which God has visited us by means of our association in this church; it is to some of us friend, nurse, mother, and home, all in one. If we sing more heartily about ourselves as recipients of divine mercy than some might think comely, we can only say that we cannot help it. If you drop in at a marriage, and there is much said at the wedding feast about the family and its history, you need not go and put it in the papers, nor even criticize the family greetings too closely. Very likely they do seem to look too exclusively at home affairs; but pray pardon them for once. Well, whether men forgive me or not, I must and will speak; but all I have to say is to ascribe every good thing unto the Lord alone, even to the God of Abraham, "the God of the whole earth shall he be called."

II. Now we will turn to a second point. In the second place, THE ENCIRCLING BLESSING OF THE DIVINE GOODNESS IS TO BE CONFESSED. The psalmist sings: "Thou crownest the year with thy goodness," as though God circled the year and put a coronet about it head, a gem for every month, a pearl for every day, a matchless crown of unceasing goodness which surrounds the whole year. Now I venture to say that the period of twenty-five years, or a whole quarter of a century, wears its crown royal even more conspicuously than any single year. From the first day even until now God has enclosed the whole time with his goodness. I make no exception. We had a dark day once when we were scattered with sorrow; but as I read the fifth verse of the psalm, it is easy to work it into our praise, "By terrible things in righteousness wilt thou answer us, O God of our salvation."

Standing happily among you, addressing you in this calm and quiet manner, I recall that night in which the multitude seemed to be taken with sudden panic and to rush madly from the house, and then we heard of dead and wounded in our congregation, and the preacher's heart was broken till he felt it would be well to die. Yet out of that calamity with all its unspeakable grief there sprang a blessing, the fruit of which we have continued still to reap. Yes, I make no exception to anything. Sick and ill oftentimes has the preacher been, but valued lessons have thus been taught to him and through him taught to the people. Sickness has fallen here and there, and sometimes affliction and poverty, but you have all of you learnt something under the rod, and you have blessed God for his fatherly discipline, fraught with eternal benefit. Yes, Lord, it is true in our case, "Thou crownest the year with thy goodness."

Now, let us just look at this all-encircling goodness of the Lord which we have seen from the first day till now.

I saw it first of all in inspiring the few brethren that met together as a church with confidence in God at the very outset. Our first meeting for prayer was, I think, more largely attended than our first sermon. The church was admonished and brought low, but the brethren prayed with great reliance upon God and showed no sign of distrust. They did not say "Die"; they did not believe in becoming extinct, but every man seemed resolved to set his face like a flint, to win prosperity at the hands of God, and for this I thank *him*. Is he not said in our psalm to be the confidence of the ends of the earth?

This confidence was the beginning of an endless chain of goodness. Then the Lord was pleased in infinite mercy to prepare men's hearts to hear the gospel. It was not possible, they said, that great places could be filled with crowds to hear the old-fashioned gospel. The pulpit had lost its power, so unbelievers told us; and yet no sooner did we begin to preach in simple strains the gospel of Christ, than the people flew as a cloud and as doves to their windows. And what listening there was at Park Street, where we scarcely had air enough to breathe! And when we got into the larger place, what attention was manifest! What power seemed to go with every word that was spoken?

I say it, though I was the preacher; for it was not I, but the grace of God which was with me. There were stricken down among us some of the most unlikely ones. There were brought into the church and added to God's people some of those that had wandered far away from the path of truth and righteousness, and these by their penitent love quickened our life and increased our zeal. The Lord gave the people more and more a willingness to hear, and there was no pause either in the flowing stream of hearers, or in the incoming of converts. The Holy Spirit came down like showers which saturate the soil till the clods are ready for the breaking; and then it was not long before we heard on the right and on the left the cry, "What must we do to be saved?" We were busy enough in those days in seeing converts, and thank God we have been so ever since. We had some among us who gave themselves up to watch for the souls for men, and we have a goodly number of such helpers now, perhaps more than ever we had; and thank God, these found and still find many souls to watch over. Still the arrows fly, and still the smitten cry out for help, and ask that they may be guided to the great healing Lord. Blessed be God's name for this. He went with us all those early days, and gave us sheaves even at the first sowing, so that we began with mercy; and he has been with us even until now, till our life has become one long harvest-home.

I am bound to acknowledge with deep thankfulness that during these twenty-five years the word has been given me to speak when the time has come for preaching. It may look to you a small thing that I should be able to come before you in due time, but it will not seem so to my brethren in the ministry who recollect that for twenty-five years my sermons have been printed as they have been delivered. It must be an easy thing to go and buy discourses at sixpence or a shilling each ready lithographed and read them off, as hirelings do, but to speak your heart out every time and yet to have something fresh for twenty-five years is no child's play. Who shall do it unless he cries unto God for help?

I read but the other day a newspaper criticism upon myself in which the writer wondered that a man should keep on year after year with so few themes, and such a narrow groove to travel in: but, my brethren, it is not so, our themes are infinite for number and fullness. Every text of Scripture is boundless in its meaning; we could preach from the Bible throughout eternity and not exhaust it. The groove narrow? The thoughts of God narrow? The divine word narrow? They know it not, for his commandment is exceeding broad. Had we to speak of politics or philosophy, we had run dry long ago, but when we have to preach the Saviour's everlasting love, the theme is always fresh, always new. The incarnate God, the atoning blood, the risen Lord, the coming glory, these are subjects which defy exhaustion. Yet bless we the Eternal Spirit who gives both seed to the sower and bread to the eater, that we have had spiritual food for our people as often as the season has come round. I must render my special note; and if at any time you have been blest by the word I have spoken, you must render your tribute too. All these years he has crowned us with his goodness by giving us the good word to preach in His name.

But, dear brethren, I am most happy to thank God for crowning the years with his goodness by helping us in the reaping and ingathering of souls. I say "us" advisedly. Here we have had a church which from the first began to seek the souls of men. If any of you do not work for

Christ I should think you have a hard time of it among us, for one or another is pretty sure to use the ox-goad upon you. Both by example and by precept, and by the general spirit of the brotherhood, idlers stand rebuked. Our brethren and sisters from the first began working for the good of men as best they could. Not in a fine, artistic manner; I do not think we ever tried that. We did it very blunderingly, but we went at it with all our hearts. Our young brethren tried their hands at teaching and preaching; very likely it was intellectually very poor preaching, but it was full of heart and it did well despite its imperfections. The teaching and the looking after converts, the trying to form new churches, the opening of prayer-meetings and all sorts of holy works were not done after any set fashion; but they were done somehow, and often done with a desperate valor and a simple faith which surprised and cheered me.

Often and often have I brushed the tears from my eyes when I have received from some here present offering for the Master's work which utterly surpassed all my ideas of giving. The consecration of their substance by some among you has been apostolic; I have known those who have so given from their poverty, that they have sometimes given all that they had, and when I have even hinted at their exceeding the bounds of prudence they have seemed hurt, and pressed the gift again for some other work of the Master whom they love. The Lord knows every one of your hearts: wherein ye have come short he knoweth and may his grace forgive; but wherein, as I most honestly bear witness, many here have gone up to the measure of their ability and even beyond it, he knows and will reward. For your zeal, and industry and consecration I must bless the Lord who crowns the years with his goodness.

There are few among you, I should think, who have worked for the master who have not seen most encouraging results in the conversions of those for whom you have cared. Certainly there are many among you between whom and myself there might pass a telegraphic glance, awakening glad memories. You have brought to me one after another souls that you have won. You wanted me to speak to them personally because you had an idea that I might be more tender than anybody else. I am afraid you think too highly of me in this respect; still I have been right glad to see those you brought to me, because they were your children. How glad I have been that, inasmuch as I brought you to Christ though his grace, when you have brought others to Christ have seemed to be a sort of grandsire in your midst, rejoicing in your joy, triumphing in your success. And I shall not exceed the truth when I say that I look upon many of you with an intense love, and satisfaction, because God has made you great winners of souls. You have not sat here to listen to me and to enjoy your Sundays, but you have been sowers of the good seed. You have many times denied yourselves the privileges of God's house that you might go and look after others, and the Lord has given you your wages.

How many of you have brought back whose feet have almost gone? How many you have helped by sweet encouragement when they have been depressed? I know not all your labours of love, but God knows. This much I know that the pastorate of this church is practically carried out by the church itself. Beloved elders labour with a diligence which I cannot too much commend, still it were impossible with five thousand persons to care for that a few men should fulfill the service. You watch over one another in the Lord, and for this I bless him, to whom must be rendered all the praise. I feel the more free to speak about what he has wrought by you and in you, because you will not take any glory to yourselves but lay it at his feet. Lord, thou hast blest us exceedingly, beyond what we asked or even thought, and in return we bless thee!

When I recollect how as a boy I stood among you and feebly began to preach of Jesus Christ, and how these twenty-five years without dissension, ay, without the dream of dissension, in perfect love compacted as one man, you have gone on from one work of God to another, and have never halted, hesitated or drawn back, I must and will bless and magnify him who hath crowned these years with his goodness.

III. Now I come to my closing point. It is this: THE CROWNING BLESSING IS CONFESSED TO BE OF GOD not only the encircling blessing but the crowning blessing.

What is the crown of a church? Well, some churches have one crown and some another. I have heard of a church whose crown was its organ, the biggest organ, the finest organ ever played, and the choir the most wonderful choir that ever was. Everybody in the district said, "Now, if you want to go to a place where you will have fine music that is the spot." Our musical friends may wear that crown if they please. I will never pluck at it or decry it; I feel no temptation in that direction. I have heard of others whose crown has been their intellect. There are very few people indeed, not as many people by one-tenth as there are sittings, but then they are such a select people, the *elite*, the thoughtful and intelligent! The ministry is such that only one in a hundred can possibly understand what is said, and the one in the hundred who does understand it is therefore a most remarkable person. That is their crown. Again I say I will not filch it. Whatever there may be that is desirable about it, the brother who wears it shall wear it all his days for me; I have heard of other crowns; amongst the rest, that of being "a most respectable church." All the people are respectable. The minister of course is respectable. I believe he is "Reverend," or "Very reverend," and everybody and thing about him is to the last degree "respectable." Fustian jackets and cotton gowns are warned off by the surpassing dignity of everything in and around the place. As for a working man, such a creature is never seen on the premises and could not be supposed to be; and if he were to come he would say, "The preacher preaches double Dutch or Greek, or something of the sort;" he would not hear language which he could understand. This is not a very brilliant crown, this crown of respectability; it certainly never flashed ambition into my soul. But our crown under God has been this, the poor have the gospel preached unto them, souls are saved, and Christ is glorified.

O my beloved church holds fast that thou hast, that no man takes this crown away from thee! As for me, by God's help, the first and last thing that I long for is to bring men to Christ. I care nothing about fine language, or about the pretty speculations of prophecy, or a hundred dainty things; but to break the heart and bind it up, to lay hold on a sheep of Christ and bring it back into the fold, is the one thing I would live for. You also are of the same mind, are you not? Well, we have had this crowning blessing that, as nearly as I can estimate; more than nine thousand persons have joined this church. If they were all alive now, or all with us now, what a company they would be. Some have fallen asleep, and many are members with other churches, working for the Master where they are probably more influential than they could have been at home. Some of our members we were glad to lose, because our loss was the gain of the universal church. We sent them out to colonize and so to increase the Master's kingdom. For which we must and will rejoice.

But another crown to any church I think is when its members are maintained in their profession. If many are added and then they are scattered again, if they do but come to go, if they are found and then straightway lost, what is the benefit of it? But this has been our crown or rejoicing, that we have seen the young converts matured in grace. The blade has become the ear, and the ear has become the full corn in the ear, for which God be thanked. And there has been this about it, that as we built together as living stones, so we have remained together. I have a great many faults, and I often wonder how it is you put up with me, but we have not thought of parting; the mortar which holds us together in the building is very binding. I am not so much surprised that I put up with you, for it is my duty and office to bear with all, and none of you have caused me grief, except such as have walked unworthily and grieved the Spirit of God; we have gone on well together under God's blessing these many years, and have no hesitation about continuing in the same loving unity.

During these twenty-five years I have had to attend to the quarrels and differences of scores of little churches where their weakness should have been the strongest argument for union. Men usually divide when they are already too few for the work, and this is a grievous evil under the sun. Churches rent with contention have laid the wretched differences before me and I have had many a heavy burden to carry while trying to set things right: but I have not had to spend one five minutes in seeking to heal a breach in this church or maintain its unity. The Lord has given us brotherly love, and unto his name be praise. Brethren who have been members of other churches where you have seen trouble, you know what a comfort it is to be connected with a church where we endeavor to walk in love to one another, and where the noise of war has not disturbed our gates. Truly I must say, and I do say it, "O Lord, thou givest peace in our borders and thou fillest us with the finest of the wheat. Thou crownest the years with thy goodness."

Nor is this all. We ought to bless God for the fruit-bearing ones that have been among us. Workers of all sorts are found for the different agencies of the church as they are required, and God has given us some whom he has honored exceedingly who are our strength for home work. But, besides that, this church has this day an army of above four hundred ministers trained at her side, who are now scattered all over the globe preaching the gospel of Jesus Christ, while as a militia we have some eighty or more colporteurs disseminating godly books.

Best of all, we have a growing band of missionaries. My heart leaped within me on Monday night when I heard the young people, and saw how one and another of our brethren were devoting themselves to mission work. This I reckon to be the brightest crown of all. If the Lord will but infuse the missionary spirit into us and force out many to go abroad to preach the gospel of Jesus Christ our cup will run over and we shall have again to say, "Praise waiteth for thee, O God, in Sion, for thou crownest the years with thy goodness."

Last of all, and never to be forgotten, during these twenty-five years there have gone from us to the upper realms about eight hundred who had named the name of Jesus. Professing their faith in Christ, living in his fear, dying in the faith, they gave us no cause to doubt their sincerity, and therefore we may not question their eternal safety. Many of them gave us in life and in death all the tokens we could ask for of their being in Christ, and therefore we sorrow not as those that are without hope. Why, when I think of them, many of them my sons and daughters now before the throne, they fill me with solemn exultation. Do you not see them in their white robes? Eight hundred souls redeemed by blood. These are only what we knew of and had enrolled. How many there may have been converted here who never joined our earthly fellowship, but, nevertheless, have gone home I cannot tell. There probably have been more than those whose names we know, if we consider the wide area over which the printed sermons circulate. They are gathering home one by one, one by one, but they make a goodly company. Our name is Gad, for "a troop cometh." Happy shall we be to overtake those who have outmatched us and entered into the promised land before us. Let us remember them, and by faith join our hands with them. Flash a thought to unite the broken family, for we are not far from them, nor are they far from us, since we are one in Christ. This too is our crown.

And now I want one thing more. There is such a thing as a greed that never is satisfied, and I have a great greed upon me now. I frankly confess my covetousness. Whenever the Lord gives us any great spiritual gift we want more, nor are we blamed for this, but bidden to covet earnestly the best gifts. This, then, is my further desire. I should be rejoiced beyond measure if on this night, and during the next two or three days in which we keep holyday, and bless the Lord for his goodness, some brethren were moved by the Holy Ghost to undertake some new work for Christ which they have not thought of before. Come, my brother, may the Lord crown this year this day with his goodness by putting it into your heart to break up new soil, and sow a fresh field for Jesus. Have you been an idler? Buckle to! Today join the laborers and leave the loiterers. Get to the Master's work. Have you been already diligent? I have more hope in appealing to you.

Brother, sister, try something more, something more tonight. Roll over in your mind what there is that is left undone in the branch of holy service for which you are fitted, or for which you might get to be fitted and engage in it. Come now. Consecrate yourself to the Lord anew tonight, and pray Him to lift you to a higher platform and into a nobler state of consecration. That would be a blessed crowning of the years with His goodness.

And what if some young men here were to say, "We shall prosper in business, no doubt, for we feel up to the mark for it. God has given us brain and skill and a fair opening, but inasmuch as we have capacity we will consecrate it." I hear the sorrows of China borne on the wailing of the wind and the sighing of the sea! Millions upon millions are perishing for lack of knowledge; will no one pity them? The need of India's teeming population cries to us in voice which pierce the heart will no one listen and help? A voice comes forth from the excellent Glory, "Whom shall I send, and who will go for us?" It were a crown to end the year with if there came from this and that set of useful, earnest Christian men the reply of individual hearts, "Here am I! Here am I! Send me!" The Lord gives us this crown!

One thing more. Oh, if some hearts would yield themselves to the Saviour tonight! If some were converted tonight, what a crown that would be to finish up these years with. Testimonial, sirs? No testimonial can ever be given to the preacher which can equal a soul converted! These are the seals of our ministry and the wages of our hire. Socrates, on his birthday, had a present given him by each of his students. Some brought less and some brought more. Among the rest there was one who had nothing in the world to bring and so he came to Socrates and said, "Master, I give you myself. I love you with all my heart." The sage judged this to be the most precious of all the tributes.

Will not some of you cry, "I do not know that I could be a missionary, or that I have any gifts, or talents or substance that I could contribute, but, Lord, I give my heart to you to be renewed by Grace"? God bring you, poor sinner, to Jesus' feet to surrender your whole nature to His sway that He may wash it in His blood, fill it with His Spirit and use it for His Glory! He says, "My son, give me your heart," and when the heart is yielded, He accepts the gift. May the Eternal Spirit lead many to give themselves thus to Jesus this night and it will be the crowning joy of all the years! Amen and amen.

6. [Monday] "Address" By C. H. Spurgeon, May 19, 1879 (*MV*)

We have been so fully absorbed in joyful praise that I would rather be silent than address you tonight; but necessity is laid upon me to do so because the papers to be read tomorrow will occupy most of the time, and there are some few things which I feel bound to say. I must crave your indulgence this evening even if we go a good deal beyond the general closing time of half-past eight. It is a special night; we have taken twenty-five years to reach it, and may now be permitted to make most of it.

I have, as you must imagine, felt the deepest emotion, at the end of these twenty-five years of your affectionate co-operation; and especially an emotion, which I shall not attempt to express, of grateful affection to you all for the noble testimonial which you have raised to commemorate the event. I felt sure that you would take up the plan as soon as it was proposed to you by the deacons; but it never entered into my heart that anything like such a testimonial as you have prepared for me could possibly have been given. The net sum which is to be handed to me is, I am informed, £6,238, the spontaneous giving, the universal giving, the delighted giving of the entire church and congregation. Everyone has seemed jealous of being excluded, and so all have pressed their gifts, rich and poor, young and old. I certainly could not have imagined that anything like such a large sum would have been raised for such an object; and yet, when I remember your many other words and deeds of love, I cannot be surprised at anything. It is just like you; your conduct to me is all of a piece and may God bless you for it.

I was ill all the while you were doing this great deed of love, and I could not rise from my bed, but each day I had tidings of some sort about you and your words and deeds of love; and I hardly knew how to bear it. It lifted me out of despondency, but it cast me down with exceeding gratitude. I hardly like to speak upon the subject, because it has been a rule with me not to take a text which I could not hope to grasp. Little boats are safest while they keep in sight of shore. This subject is one of those upon which the more said the better, and yet it remains better than all that can be condense my sermon into a sentence and that sentence is a prayer: May the God whom I serve bless you all a thousand fold for this token of your love and kindness towards me, which I know you have rendered for Christ's sake.

An evil has come upon me therefore at this period that I have to speak about myself. Last night I had a very difficult task. I felt that I must praise God for these twenty-five years of mercies, and I earnestly endeavored to avoid all self-praise; but being personally mixed up with all this blessedness I was compelled to become a fool in glorying. I did not like the task, and I felt glad when it was over; and I feel very much the same to-night; and yet I must speak to my Lord's praise even though I am a fool. What he has done by our ministry on this spot is not gathered up in this place, no, not a thousandth part of it; nor is the influence that has gone forth with the sermons and other works confined to you, nor to a hundred times as many as you. No, there is scarcely a place on the face of the earth where our mother tongue is spoken where the word of God, as sounded forth from this house, has not reached. In the bush of Australia and the backwoods of America, at the Cape of Good Hope and in the cities of India, I have at this moment hundreds of readers, among whom are many who have been led to Christ by the sermons.

Now, in this, I cannot take any honour to myself, for I must say with the apostle, "Though I preach the gospel: I have nothing to glory of, for necessity is laid upon me; yea, woe is unto me, if I preach not the gospel!" I could not help preaching the gospel. I could not live without preaching the gospel. If any other man has a diviner message than Christ's Holy Gospel, let him by all means declare it; but as I know of nothing a hundredth part as good, nothing that so cheers and sustains my own spirit, and nothing which can work such wonders in men's hearts and lives, I must go on with the old, old story, as long as my tongue can move; I cannot help preaching, and therefore I do not desire to be praised for doing what is as necessary to me as taking breath.

In looking back through the whole of those twenty-five years, I observe that everything I have ever done, comes under this same law of necessity; I have done nothing aright except under a constraint which I do not wish to resist. First of all I came to New Park Street Chapel to be your pastor. It was no choice of mine, I neither sought it nor wished it and yet no one will deny that I was bound to come when I saw so grand an opening for usefulness. Who could have refused to enter where so wide a door was open? When the chapel became too small, I could not help it; the people would come though you can bear me witness that I told them to keep to their own ministers and not to come crowding out the sinners. Then we went to Exeter Hall, and filled that well-known edifice. Some have praised me for setting the fashion of preaching in these public buildings but really I had no idea of doing any such thing; we simply went into that hall because there was no other place to go to. We could not help it.

I recollect going with Mr. William Olney to see the Surrey Music Hall, and thinking what a vast building it was, wondering whether it could be filled with hearers. One or two of our good members thought it wrong to go to what they persisted in calling, "the devil's house." I did not agree with their hard names, but encouraged them to stop away and not to violate their consciences. At the same time I bade them not to discourage either their brethren or me, for we were willing to go even into the devil's house to win souls. We did not go the Music Hall because we thought that it was a good thing to worship in places of amusement, but because we had no other place to go to. Here again if I did well it was because I could help it.

In due time this Tabernacle was built because we could not help it; we must have a place to house the people and to carry on our work. We were driven to build because no fit place could be hired, and driven to pay for it because I could not live in debt. This spacious house was erected from sheer necessity because we could not help it.

Then the College was commenced because there were some young men preaching the gospel, and some of them made stupids of themselves. I believe that one of them is here, and I hope he will not take the remark as personal, though I dare say if he does he will give a nod of assent. They *would* preach whether trained or not, and we did not want it to be said that they came from us, and talked sheer nonsense, and so we thought that as our young men would preach, the best thing would be to give them an opportunity of learning how to do their work a little better. Hence sprang the College at the first and God has sent me men from time to time whom I could not refuse and he has sent the means to educate them and so I could not help going on with this form of service.

When a devoted lady, till then unknown to me, sent me a letter to say that she had laid aside £20,000 for an Orphanage, who, in his sense, could help accepting the trust and starting the Orphanage? I being in my senses and having a heart could not refuse the care of these dear boys. Thus always and ever have I been pressed on from behind, no, I think from above, by a strong influence or other which has carried me along with it in willing submissiveness. I do not think that I have ever sketched or schemed or devised anything; but everything has shaped itself. I have not tugged an oar willfully against the stream of providence, but my little boat has floated on and on, borne along by a current of which I was not the creator, but the willing subject. I have rejoiced to be energetically active and yet to feel myself as much overborne by necessity as if I had been passive. In nothing whatever can I take the slightest honour to myself because I say again almost in the apostle's words: Necessity was laid upon me, yea, and woe was unto me if I did not thus serve the Lord.

The like necessity had founded and maintained the Almshouses, the Colportage and the Society of Evangelists: these could not be prevented and needed no plotting or scheming, necessity was laid upon me.

Moreover, friends, I have one, among many reasons, for speaking with bated breath as to anything which God has wrought by me, because in my heart of hearts I am made to feel that the true honour belongs to unknown helpers, who serve the Lord and yet have none of the credit of having done so. I cannot help being public, but I envy those who have done good by stealth and have refused to have their names so much as whispered. I do not think I ever told in public this fact, which will ever live in my memory. This great house was to be built, and some £30,000 would be wanted. We did not know when we started that it would be so much; we thought about £12,000 or £15,000 would suffice, and we felt that we were rather bold to venture upon that. When we came to the undertaking of responsibilities there was a natural shrinking on the part of the committee with which we started. No one could be blamed, it was a great risk, and personally I did not wish any one to undertake it; I was quite prepared for any risk but then I had no money of my own, and so was a mere man of straw. I say there was a measure of fear and trembling, but I had none. I was as sure upon the matter as possible and reckoned upon paying all the cost. This quiet assurance, however, had a foundation which reflects credit upon one who has for some years gone to his reward.

When I was riding with a friend to preach in the country, a gentleman overtook us and asked me if I would get out of the trap and ride with him in the gig, as he wished to speak to me. I did so. He said, "You have got to build that big place." I said, "Yes." He said, "You will find that many friends will feel nervous over it. Now, as a business man,

I am sure you will succeed, and besides that God is with the work, and it cannot fail. I want you never to feel nervous or downcast about it." I told him that it was a great work and that I hoped the Lord would enable me to carry it through. "What do you think," he said, "will be required, at the outside, to finish it off altogether?" I said, "£20,000 must do it in addition to what we have." "Then," he said, "I will let you have the £20,000, on the condition that you shall only keep what you need of it to finish the building". "Mark," he said, "I do not expect to give more than £50; but you shall have bonds and leases to the full value of £20,000 to fall back upon." This was royal. I told no one, but the ease of mind this act gave me was of the utmost value. I had quite as much need of faith for I resolved that none of my friend's money should be touched, but I had no excuse for fear. God was very good to me, but by this fact I was disabled from all personal boasting. My friend gave his £50, and no more, and I felt deeply thankful to him for the help which he would have rendered had it been required. There were others who did like generous deeds, and among them was the giver of £5,000, and the late Mr. Joynson, and his friends, by whose means we saw our way to purchase the freehold. I must mention also Mr. Higgs, who erected the building so well and so cheaply, and our departed brother, Mr. Cook, who was Secretary of the movement. If there be honors let these wear them.

Then, in regard to the Orphanage; the origin of that blessed institution is due, under God, to that Christian woman who keeps herself so entirely behind the scenes; the carrying of it out is due to my co-trustees and the head-master and other people behind me who do the work. In the building of the College, a dear friend gave £3,000 in one sum, but desires never to be named, yet the fact ought never to be forgotten. I have no wish to wear borrowed plumes, and, therefore, I must give honour to which honour is due, and all I can honestly keep for myself is that it is under my lead that others do so well. I have always confessed that I am simply the weather-beaten and uncomely figure-head of this gallant ship; I go first though the waves, but there is a grand power behind me which urges me on, and this works mightily though one and another and in general though you all.

When I have been able to bestow large gifts towards new chapels it has been a great joy to give of my own substance, but you must not think that I have ever had the personal means to give all that has been put down to me, but I have acted as the agent of one or two who have wished to help me and have made no condition but that I would not mention their names. Those are the men to whom honour is due if we poor mortals may even talk of honour at all. Here, too, are my other dear helpers around me, to whom my deepest gratitude is given because they never want pressing to work. I have only to express a wish that such a work should be done, and they will have no stone unturned to do it. Whether they would have done so much without me I will not conjecture, but I am sure that I could not have achieved success without *them*. Let God be praised for raising up willing helpers for that great work to which you and I have alike consecrated our all.

Bear with me if I say that twenty-five years' leadership over such a church as this has not been without its sore difficulties. I do not think that many of you know me at all, nor do I wonder, for I do not know myself yet. It is generally supposed that I preach with very little trouble or effort. Now, while I rejoice to say that as a rule preaching is a source of the greatest delight when I am once fully engaged in it, yet my deacons are witnesses that for years I never entered this pulpit without such a fit of trembling and distress of mind that sickness of the most violent kind came upon me. Although, thanks to my excellent door-keeper, Mr. Murrel, to whom we all owe a far greater debt of gratitude than we are aware of, I am now free from the fear of the crowd, yet the prospect of preaching is not often a pleasant one to me. Often have I felt that I would sooner be flogged than face the crowd again.

It remains with me as at the first, a venture from which I shrink with a kind of dread, although when once I have begun it is an intense joy to preach. I asked a good brother minister some years ago whether he knew this feeling and if so, whether it was to be got over. He said that he was afraid that he had outgrown the feeling; "but," he said, "I hope you never will. I hope you will always feel an overwhelming emotion, for when you do not your power in preaching will be gone." This witness is true. When our message stirs our very soul it is likely to stir the souls of others, but if we are unfeeling so will our hearers be. I have not preached as I ought to have done, but I have thrown my whole heart into it, and I have been stirred through and through with a desire to impress the truth upon my audience. It has never seemed to me to be a small matter to address such an audience as has been gathered in this house. I do feel more and more at home in speaking from the same spot, to the same beloved people; but then the trial only takes another form and while there is not so much fear just before preaching, there is far more labour and anxiety in striving to get the right subject, and to get one's soul into sympathy with it. To bring forth the right topics and to make these interesting from year to year has cost me more effort than some might imagine. My happy task is one which taxes my physical, mental and spiritual nature to the uttermost.

In addition to this, during the time that I have been preaching the gospel in this place, I have suffered many times from severe sickness and frightful mental depression, sinking almost to despair. Almost every year I have been laid aside for a season; for flesh and blood cannot bear the strain, at least such flesh and blood as mine. I believe that affliction was necessary to me and has answered salutary ends; but I would, if it were God's will, escape from such frequent illness: that must be according to his will and not mine. If I should grow worse and worse, and be even more frequently unwell, have patience with me. If I should in future years show more serious marks of wear and tear, be content if I am not always in my place, for I always will be at my post when I can. And when, at last, it comes to pass that I am too often ill, or altogether too infirm, I hope I shall have the grace to be the first to perceive the fact and shall be ready at once to leave the position to an abler occupant.

I cannot be sure of doing this, for many old ministers have been very tenacious of their office and I may become the same. Just now, however, we need not talk of this, for, as the proverb hath it, "there is life in the old dog yet." And I may by degrees mend and improve, and get over my physical trouble and perhaps be much more hale and hearty in days to come than I have been for years. Who knows? My God grant me this high favor. My great joy in all this time has been that in the church we have had no serious troubles of any kind. We have had no division upon doctrines or ordinances. I have sometimes heard a rumour that some one brother has been heretical on a certain point, but it never came in my way so that I knew it to be a fact, or if I did, it was after the wanderer had found it best to go elsewhere.

I never thought that it was my business to go about, like a terrier dog sniffing for rats to find out everybody who was a little queer in his thinking. To the best of my knowledge and belief, the whole company, with scarcely half-a-dozen exceptions have remained faithful to the orthodox faith and to the old-fashioned truths of the gospel. Thus we have wasted no time in controversy, but have had for our motto, "One Lord, one faith, one Baptism," and in that same unity we are still held. Nor have I had many great trials as to the practice of the church members. We have not been without our share of shameful hypocrites, and sad apostates, who have gone out from us because they were not of us; and have brought disgrace upon the name of Christ. We never expected that we should be without these, for the gospel net gathers fishes of many kinds. But yet when I think of the devotion, the consecration, the liberality, and the holiness of the great mass of the membership, I can only bless, and praise, and magnify the name of the Lord, whose Holy Spirit has wrought all our works in us.

Most heartily do I bless God that you have been so united. It may be that one friend has differed from another upon some unimportant point, but no one has allowed such difference to mar our unity. Our work has been one and so have our hearts been. Toward me the kind feeling has been very fervent, and I have been treated with far greater respect than I ever wished for. When one or two have been irritated I have always tried to remove the grievance, and no sooner have I attended it than they have responded, and the matter has ended. I have had no policy, and as a church we have made no rules. We seek to judge each case on its own merits by the law of love, and it is to me a first principle to give way to the uttermost where no principle is involved.

To think evil of no one is my earnest desire, and to do good to all men is my hearty ambition. Love is power and all other heat is weakness. As a matter of experience, I have found that men are seldom are as bad as they are painted, and that Christian men have always more virtues than they are credited with. God's people are not perfect by a long way: if they were they would not want us to minister to them, but when we get amongst them we try to turn their bright side uppermost, and to utilize the best part of their character. Tradesmen put the best side of their goods foremost in their windows, and what might be questionable as a trick of trade I advocate as a law of morals: you should always look at the best side of everybody and say, "This man has an awkward corner, and if I put him to do such and such a work, he will knock against others; but I will help him to another sphere and then we shall see his nobler qualities." So have I found it and in looking round on my officers, workers, and helpers, I am more than satisfied with my comrades. Best of all the Holy Spirit has been among us keeping us alive as to divine things and hence we have been on the alert in our Master's service, and constantly making progress and this has been the main bond of our union from the first even unto this day. One service for one Lord has welded us into one mass.

There are very many things which I might be expected to say, and wherein justice, kindness, or gratitude might require a thing to be said, please take it all as said, for I have no reason for withholding anything, nor any feeling but that of open-hearted confidence and pleasure. I shall simply make a remark about the testimonial. My dear brethren, the deacons, said from the very first that there ought to be a testimonial to ME *personally*, I mean for my own use. But I said that it was God who had wrought so graciously with us, and therefore I would have nothing to do with a testimonial to me unless it could be used in his service. We thought of the alms-women, whose support has drawn so heavily upon our poor funds, and I felt that it would be of the utmost service to the church if we could raise an endowment for the support of our poor sisters. We have built rooms but have not provided the weekly pensions and I thought that it would be a good thing to put this matter out of hand. £5,000 was suggested as the amount and to this object £5,000 will go. But you have contributed £6,200, and my excellent deacons then said, "That extra £1,200 is clearly meant for you. The friends will be disappointed if you do not take it and use it for yourself."

I have been considerably scolded by several friends, who have declared that they would have given much more if some personal benefit had accrued to me. I am, however, obstinate in this matter, and it shall be even as I said at the first, that the whole of your generous offering shall go to the carrying on the work of the Lord among you. It is to God that the honour belongs and to God shall the whole of your offering go, with this exception that I wish to raise a memorial in the Almshouses to Dr. Rippon, the founder, and to add to it the record of the way in which the Almshouses were extended and endowed; and in addition there is this much for myself, I said that I should like to have in my house a piece of bronze, which should be a memorial of your abiding love. This clock, with candelabra as side ornaments, will stand in my study, and will gladden me, as it calls you to remembrance. This I shall greatly treasure and I do not doubt that one or other of my sons will treasure it after me: they are so nearly of an age, and so equal in all respects that either of them is worthy to be heir to his father's valuables.

The rest of the money shall be devoted to various purposes, some of which I shall name tomorrow, but I shall leave the amount in the hands of Mr. Thomas Olney and Mr. [T.] Greenwood, who are the treasurers, and they will see that it is so used; so that all may know and be assured that not a penny comes to me, but I shall draw it from them for the different objects as it is wanted. I shall have the credit of having received this large sum, and I shall have a corresponding number of begging letters to get it out of me, and that will be my personal gain. I dare say you have all heard that "Spurgeon makes a good thing of this Tabernacle." Well, whenever anybody hints that to you, you may on my authority assure them that I do. I should not like anybody to think that my Master does not pay his servants well. He loads us with benefits, and I am perfectly satisfied with his wages: but if the assertion is made that by my preaching in this place I have make a purse for myself, I can refer them to those who know me and my way of life among you. "Ah, but, they say, he has had a testimonial of £6,000 presented to him." Yes, he has had it, and he thanks everybody for it. Perhaps there are some other persons who would like the same testimonial, and I wish they may get it and do the same with it as I have done.

Legacies left to me and sums subscribed for the Orphanage and College and so on are spoken of as if I had some private interest in them, whereas I have neither a direct nor indirect pecuniary interest in any of these works to the amount of a penny a year. With regard to all thing else from the first day until now, I have acted on no other principle but that of perfect consecration to the work whereunto I am called. I have no riches. I sometimes wish that I had, for I could use money in an abundance of profitable ways. What have I gained of late years in my ministry here? I have gained all that I wished by way of salary, but I have for years expended almost all of it in the cause of God, and in some years even more than all. As far as my pastoral office is concerned, the net proceeds to me, after giving my share to all holy service, is not much that any man need envy me. Yet this is not your fault, nor any one's fault, it is my joy and delight to have it so.

The Lord is a good and a gracious paymaster; and inasmuch as men say, "Doth Spurgeon serve God for naught?" Spurgeon replies "No, he is paid a thousand times over and finds it a splendid thing to be in the service of the Lord Jesus." If anyone will serve the Lord Jesus Christ after the same or a better fashion he too will make the same splendid thing of it; he shall have splendid opportunities for working from morning till night, and far into the night on many an occasion; splendid openings for giving away as much as he can earn, splendid opportunities of finding happiness in making other people happy, and easing the sorrows of others by entering into hearty sympathy with them.

Brethren, hitherto the Lord hath helped us! That clock shall, each time it ticks, be a memorial of divine help. Its many wheels and one result shall image our unity and its practical effect and its lasting metal will, I hope, be the emblem of the perpetuity of our love in Christ Jesus. For many a year may we remain as united as we now are. May the Lord enable us to go on as we have done, and to do more and better by his grace. Good men were here when I first came, but these have passed away one by one and there has been raised up among us another race of equally faithful men and I rejoice to see yet another generation rising up to succeed the present.

Dear names of honored brethren will occur to you, "familiar in your mouths as household words," men and women who were our delight; but when these went home the gaps in our ranks filled up, and the army remained complete. No minister ever had a better set of friends than I have at this moment, and this I say, when as you all know, I should not hesitate for a moment to say the contrary if it were true. To my mind I have around me the pick and cream of men. I wish they were all better, and myself much better; but I cannot tell in what respects I could have them altered so as to improve upon them. I cannot wish for kinder friends, or heartier helpers, or more earnest workers than I have in all departments. Then, let us thank God, there are more coming up to keep the good cause alive. We are not going to indulge the foolish idea that anybody is essential to God's work, neither pastor nor co-pastor, nor deacon, nor elder. Others will come to the front when we flag; in fact, for myself, if not for the rest of my comrades, I begin to see where successors are preparing by God's gracious forethought.

I rejoice in this that the wealthier friends of this church do not find their sons going off to the Church of England and other fashionable churches, and leaving us. It is said that as soon as families rise in the world they get too proud to be Baptists, but it has not been so among us. Our young gentlemen are with us as their fathers are, and I have not the slightest doubt, that they will follow their fathers in the work of the Lord Jesus Christ, and be our strength for many years to come. We have no trace, so far as I can see of the "respectability" disease among us. God has kept us clear of that cause of defection in the silly ones, and here instead of the fathers shall be the children whom thou mayest make princes in all the earth.

Let us go forward, brethren, let us go forward. We have made a very fair beginning in God's strength, and to him be the honour of it, but I regard tonight not as the goal, but as the starting place we have only laid the fire, it will get alight soon. We have truly laid underground foundations of a structure which now we trust will rise into open day. Here is one point for a new departure. Listen and consider it. A day or two ago, the lady who founded the boys' orphanage, sent me £50 for the girls' orphanage. I answered somewhat to this effect. "I am very grateful for the proposal, but at the same time, I am not very well, and the times are not very hopeful, and therefore I had rather not begin any new work just yet. I proposed to keep the £50 in case we did build for girls, and if not to put it over to the boys." "No," said our friend, "You are right in your judgment, but take the £50 as the first brick; for I am fully assured that many more bricks will shortly be added." Now I propose that £50 of the testimonial should be placed with my dear friend's £50 that we may found the girls' orphanage together.

I will not say more because she never has been outdone, and I do not think ever will be. I do not mean to press this new enterprise just now, but only to moot it and see whereunto this thing will grow. Other eggs will come to the nest egg, and the nest will become full, and then we shall have another family of little chicks. I feel as though I was laying the first stone of the girls' orphanage, and you were all saying "go ahead." This is a good note for our present page of history, "second twenty-five years of pastorate commenced by the inauguration of project for girls' orphanage." "What next?" says somebody. I cannot tell you what next, but, you see, I am driven to this girls' orphanage. I have this £50 forced upon me, and I cannot get rid of it. Would you have me refuse to use this for poor fatherless girls? No, your hearts would not so counsel me. Thus, you see, of my own free will, compelled by constraining grace, I accept a further charge and look to see prayer and faith open a new chapter of marvels.

Do not persuade yourselves, dear friends that you have done enough. I do not know how I could preach on that text just yet. If our Lord Jesus, who loved us, and who gave himself for us, and to whom we are everlastingly debtors, were to say to us, "I will give you no more to do," we should reply, "Nay, Master, deal not so with us, but favor us with thy kind commissions. As long as Thou wilt accept our services, here we are. Only give us strength and grace and we will labour to the honour and praise of thy holy name."

Now, I have been rambling all over the world, and forgetting many things which should have been said. I intended to say a good deal about my brother and his great help to me in pastoral oversight and about every deacon by name, but none of these need letters of commendation from me; their record is on our hearts. We are all as one man and I am part and parcel of all of you. There is Mr. Charlesworth, who is the Orphanage incarnate, and yet the Orphanage is none the less but all the more mine. There is the College, of which Mr. Rogers has been the front and pillar together with Messrs. Grace and Fergusson, but the College is all my own. There is the Colportage with its diligent Secretary and Committee, and of this I am a living member. There are the Evangelists, silver trumpet and all, and these too are mine. Our work is one, and we are one in Christ, our Lord. I will not therefore attempt to divide to any of you the praise to which you are entitled, because we are all agreed that so long as the good works go on well we do not want anybody to waste time in commending us.

We are all members of one body and mutually dependent. I am in some respects the tongue of the body, and truly I cannot say to you who are the hearing ear, "I have no need of thee," nor to you who are the who are the giving hand "I have no need of thee," nor to you who are the overseeing eye, "I have no need of thee," nor even to you afflicted ones who are the weary feet, "I have no need of thee." Brethren, I have need of you all: need of your prayers, your labours, and your love. The Lord being with us, we shall see greater things than these. Difficulties will vanish and marvels will be accomplished if we have faith in God and zeal for his glory. Again I set the standard a little further into the enemy's country and with gratitude for the past, delight in the present, and hope for the future. I would speak to the children of Israel that they *go forward*.

As we close these twenty-five years we ascribe unto the glorious Jehovah all honour and praise for ever and ever. "O give thanks unto the Lord, for he is good, for his mercy endureth forever."

[The meeting was closed in prayer by the Pastor, and the people went on their way rejoicing and singing unto the Lord whose mercy endureth forever.]

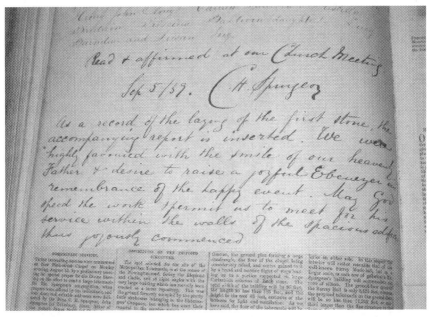

Affirming the minutes of the church meeting September 5, 1859

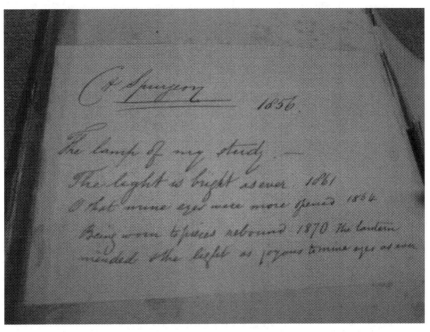

C. H. Spurgeon's Journal

C. H. Spurgeon's Tomb West Norwood Cemetery

Metropolitan Tabernacle

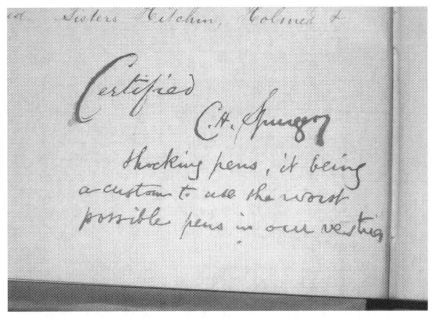

One of Spurgeon's entries in the church minutes

Spurgeon at Spurgeon's College, London

C.H. SPURGEON'S First Words at the Tabernacle

I WOULD PROPOSE THAT THE SUBJECT OF THE MINISTRY IN THIS HOUSE, AS LONG AS THIS PLATFORM SHALL STAND, & AS LONG AS THIS HOUSE SHALL BE FREQUENTED BY WORSHIPPERS, SHALL BE THE PERSON OF **JESUS CHRIST.** I AM NEVER ASHAMED TO AVOW MYSELF A CALVINIST, I DO NOT HESITATE TO TAKE THE NAME OF BAPTIST; BUT IF I AM ASKED WHAT IS MY CREED, I REPLY, "IT IS JESUS CHRIST." MY VENERATED PREDECESSOR, DR. GILL, HAS LEFT A BODY OF DIVINITY, ADMIRABLE & EXCELLENT IN ITS WAY; BUT THE BODY OF DIVINITY TO WHICH I WOULD PIN & BIND MYSELF FOR EVER, GOD HELPING ME, IS NOT HIS SYSTEM, OR ANY OTHER HUMAN TREATISE; BUT CHRIST JESUS, WHO IS THE SUM & SUBSTANCE OF THE GOSPEL, WHO IS IN HIMSELF ALL THEOLOGY, THE INCARNATION OF EVERY PRECIOUS TRUTH, THE ALL-GLORIOUS PERSONAL EMBODIMENT OF THE WAY, THE TRUTH, & THE LIFE.

Spurgeon's First Words at the Metropolitan Tabernacle

The author by Spurgeon's pulpit table

Part II
Testimonial Meeting, History, and Presentation of the Testimonial

7. Testimonial Meeting, May 20, 1879 (*MV*)

On Tuesday afternoon, May 20th, tea was provided for as many of the contributors to the Bazaar and Testimonial Fund as could be accommodated in the lecture-hall and school-rooms. At half-past six o'clock the Tabernacle was crowded in every part for the meeting at which the testimonial was to be presented. The pastor was in the chair; hymns – "Sing a hymn to Jesus," and "There is a land of pure delight," . . . were sung by the whole congregation led by the evangelistic choir; and the orphan boys sang, "I was glad when they said unto me let us go unto the house of the Lord." Prayer was offered by the chairman and Pastor W. Stott, after which Mr. Spurgeon said: "Dear friends, I do not rise to make a speech, but just to say two or three introductory words by way of starting the meeting. First, I am delighted to see a great company of you here to-night and such a representative company too, because here are not only members of our own church, and members of the churches whose pastors belong to the College, but also members of I do not know many churches in the neighbourhood, and hosts of country friends, and all sorts of good people. I am glad to see you all here to-night: may the blessing of God be upon you. I shall probably be the person who will be most uneasy in this meeting; for many reasons I am already the most thankful; for many more reasons I shall be the most thankful; for many more reasons I shall be the most thankful when it is all over. We have no time to spare, and must be use our minutes economically. First, we shall listen to a paper by our old friend and esteemed deacon, Mr. B. W. Carr, upon the history of the church during the past twenty-five years. As to the writing of that paper I gave him only one instruction, and that was that he was not to say any more about me than he was obliged to do. Whether or not he has transgressed that canon I will leave you to judge, but he has such a love for me that I should not wonder but what he will go too far upon that point and if he does I cannot help it, I am powerless to stop him. I know my own unworthiness, but I cannot help your loving me, and I know you do, for the proofs are abundant and overwhelming: you must then have liberty for this once to express your kind thoughts, and so must Mr. Carr. After some singing and short speeches Dr. Stanford will follow. You know with what sweet wisdom, with what gracious unction, and with what tender force he always writes and speaks. I feel very thankful to him that in his great weakness of bodily health he should venture to render us this noble service, and I am sure if there should be any failure in his voice you who sit in the far corners will *feel* what he is saying, even if you do not hear at all. Mr. William Olney will then have something to say about the testimonial, and other things will follow as time and opportunity offer; but first let us heartily sing our new version of "'All hail the power of Jesus' name.'"

This having been sung with wonderful power, Mr. Spurgeon said: "Those who are old like myself can remember that Mr. Carr read a paper, an excellent historical paper, at the laying of the foundation stone of this Tabernacle, and it is therefore peculiarly appropriate that he should again take up his parable and exercise his office of historian to the Tabernacle church by epitomizing these last twenty-five years."

8. "A Grateful Retrospect"

By B. W. Carr [Deacon and Historian, Metropolitan Tabernacle], May 20, 1879 (*MV*)

THE BAPTIZED CHURCH OF CHRIST, *meeting in New Park Street Chapel, Southwark*, had already enjoyed continuous tokens of the Divine favour for the space of two centuries when our present Pastor, Mr. C. H. SPURGEON, made his first visit to us in the autumn of 1853. Her ministers had been men of renown, whose names are still fragrant. Her testimony to the purity of gospel doctrine and the simplicity of Christian ordinances had been consistently maintained through successive generations. Her works of faith and labours of love had always kept in the van of evangelical enterprise. The last of the five pastors who lived and died in her midst had for sixty years been a foremost champion of religious and civil liberty and an earnest promoter of missionary enterprise at home and abroad. After the death of Dr. John Rippon, a dark cloud hovered over the Church for sixteen years. Though a few attached families clung to her fellowship, and she preserved her nominal status in the denomination, there was no palpable accession to her ranks and the influence she had been wont to exert was gradually waning. While her elder members were one by one gathered to their fathers, the younger ones were seeking residences in the outer suburbs of the metropolis. "Horselydown" and "Carter Street Lane, Bermondsey" were cherished traditions with which "New Park Street" was unable to compete.

During these sixteen years, three pastors had come and gone, all good men and true, none of them finding there a congenial sphere of labour. The cause of depression was obvious. Compelled to remove from the populous neighbourhood in which the Church had once thrived, the site selected for the handsome new Chapel on the southern bank of the Thames, above Southwark Bridge, was at so considerable a distance from the main thoroughfare of the Borough, that it required extraordinary attractions to draw a congregation. Joseph Angus was a young man of more than average scholarship and solidity of character, whose talents drew the attention of leading members of the Baptist fellowship. His subsequent career as Secretary of the Missionary Society and President of Regent's Park College has abundantly justified the estimate they formed of his intellectual abilities. James Smith, who succeeded him, was a sound, simple, sincere preacher, whose sermons were edifying and whose numerous little books were widely popular. To literature he could lay no claim; but in personal piety and practical fidelity to the sacred calling of a gospel minister he was never lacking. He came to us from Cheltenham, and to Cheltenham he afterwards returned, there to finish his course with joy. For a brief interval William Walters occupied the pulpit, but finding another field of labour, for which he was more fit, he withdrew, and in several provincial towns he has ably sustained the great principles cherished by the Baptist denomination.

The summer of 1853 was a season of anxious thought and instant prayer at New Park Street Chapel. The Sabbath Services have left no such traces in our memory as the Monday Evening Prayer Meetings. It was in answer to importunate supplication rather than to diligent enquiry that Mr. Spurgeon suddenly appeared among us. He came as a stranger, of whose fame we had never heard, of whose very name we were previously ignorant. But he was no adventurer; for the seal of heaven had already been set on his commission to preach the gospel. The charm of his youth was greatly enhanced by the maturity of his judgment. Early in life he had imbibed that creed of the orthodox fathers and that spirit of the Puritan confessors of both of which he has subsequently proved himself such an unswerving champion.

Mr. Spurgeon had but recently completed his nineteenth year when he occupied the pulpit of New Park Street Chapel for the first time. His popularity in London dates from the services of that Lord's Day. After preaching two or three alternate Sundays, he commenced his stated labours for what was arranged to be probation of three months, though it proved to be the inauguration of a pastorate that has already extended over twenty-five years.

The guidance of divine providence in the union of pastor and people was very conspicuous on the outset. To this Church he came as a man specially raised up by God to preserve her old landmarks inviolate, to foster her cherished traditions, and to lead her forward, when great advances, rapid marches, and fresh acquisitions, became imperative to keep pace with the remarkable changes that were peacefully revolutionizing the age. To the young pastor himself his new sphere of ministry had a singular fascination. He found no small pressure in often quoting from Dr. Gill, as *his sainted predecessor*. For his writings he entertained such a genuine admiration that we observe young Spurgeon's name three years prior to his coming to London among the original subscribers to Mr. Doudney's re-issue of the Doctor's famous Commentary on the Scriptures. And it is scarcely less remarkable that when facing with solemn awe the heavy responsibilities of the office he had just undertaken he made pathetic reference to a memorable and almost prophetic prayer of Dr. John Rippon, remembered by the old members as of a solitary link connecting the aged pastor with the new Chapel, "that it would please God to call, to anoint, and to commission a young minister who peradventure was not then born to be a witness for his gospel and a leader of his flock, whose successful career should throw the grateful annals of the past into the shade."

Most certainly we can now testify to the glory of God, that we have seen with our eyes and heard with our ears mightier works in the triumph of the gospel during the quarter of a century that has just transpired, than we were ever told by our forefathers of the two centuries that preceded it. The blessing had not to be long waited for when our beloved pastor settled in our midst. While throngs gathered to his ministry, multitudes were added to the Church. The little remnant thus grew into a large congregation and in his experience the history of David was in a measure reiterated, "For at that time day by day there came to him to help him, until it was a great host, like the host of God."

Mr. Spurgeon's accession to the pastorate was not the signal for a sudden convulsion, although its immediate result was a great expansion in all departments of Christian ministry and church fellowship. No changes were introduced into the conduct of the ordinary services; no innovations were made in the system of church government; no accessories of any kind were sought. Our pastor's tastes were simple, so were his manners and his speech; and yet, as if by a magic touch; there was a change conspicuous to every worshipper. The *common prayer* was instinct with life, till petitions to the Almighty were offered with an importunity that raised questionings where they did not rouse sympathy. The singing of hymns he watched with jealous care, not to realize any high standard of artistic effect, but to make them a register of faith and feeling. The *accustomed reading* of *the Scriptures* he enlivened with brief, racy expositions that served at once to clear the sense and point the moral. *Of his sermons* we need say little, because the early date at which they began to be published enables any one to acquaint him with their style. At that time they were startling, because they bore a strong contrast with the formal essays then in fashion. To our idea they showed an air of originality by no means eccentric. It is not difficult now to detect the classic models he began to study. John Bunyan, Richard Baxter, William Bridge, Richard Sibbes, and Joseph Caryl may we have been his youthful favourites; but he soon learned to make his own allegories, frame his own similitudes and to draw his pictures from nature instead of copying from the great Masters. As however, "genius," at this advanced period of the world's history, is rather conspicuous for its combinations than for its creations, so Mr. Spurgeon's sermons baffled the criticisms of the press by a peculiar blending of colors.

But the public has since grown familiar with a style which at first seemed singular and fantastic. Some carped at his dogmatism, other complained of his drollery. Dogmatic he was, for he stuck to his text as an axiom that must not be challenged; his divisions were mapped out with mathematical precision, and he interpreted the Scriptures with such deference to orthodoxy, that he often grew rather warm in his declamations, and yet he *was* very lively in his preaching. After carefully preparing his outline, he committed himself to the current, diving into his subject, and dashing about fearlessly in deep water. His masterly expositions were made palatable by quaint similes and racy anecdotes and his manly appeals to the conscience of his hearers were clothed in *market* language. He looked, as he doubtless felt, at home in the pulpit or on the platform. The peculiarity of his manner was the total absence of mannerism. In those days this natural simplicity drew a good deal of notice, for then it was accounted the duty of a minister to be decently sanctimonious, and to be thoroughly proper he must be a little dignified. But as Mr. Spurgeon never courted the clerical profession for its respectability so he looked with scorn on every semblance of affectation.

The first object on which he set his heart was to gain the ear of the public, and having once succeeded, he lost no opportunity of taking advantage of this coveted privilege to further the ends of his ministry. By the publication of a sermon once a week, the melodies and harmonies he has struck Sabbath after Sabbath have found echoes in many hearts that he could not otherwise have reached. The fire which is kindled in the pulpit does not cool in passing through the press. As tracts, these sermons are welcomed, because they state every phase of the gospel with simplicity and *naiveté* enough to attract promiscuous readers. At family devotion they often do the duty of chaplain in numerous households. In distant colonies they supply the place of minister or missionary. Wherever the Saxon tongue is spoken they circulate; and they brave the peril of translation into other tongues, without utterly destroying the vital energy. Grateful acknowledgments of their converting and edifying power are frequently addressed to him from remote regions as well as from nearer neighborhoods. In their compact form they have already accumulated into twenty-four annual volumes, and while their main purpose is to testify of Christ they also reflect much of the history of the period, mirroring, as they do, the sensations of the people and the heaving of men's hearts, when the current of popular feeling has risen high in times of national calamity or of patriotic enthusiasm. Things almost forgotten grow once again familiar as we scan the homilies that were improvised at the hour of their occurrence.

As we remember Mr. Spurgeon at the opening of his career in London, and have followed him through his entire subsequent course, we are deeply impressed with the purity of character he has maintained, while amidst difficulties and dangers his fame has expanded to a worldwide reputation. In idiosyncrasy he may have lost much, but he has gained more than he has lost, and he has kept all that was worth keeping. The rawness that once grated on the palate of the fastidious has developed into ripeness. He is less like John the Baptist crying in the wilderness than he used to be, but he is far more like Jesus Christ teaching in the synagogues. Highly cultured by the study of books old and new, by converse with Christians of other fellowships than our own, by solitary hours of communion with him who is invisible and by frequent seasons of patient suffering he has gained a rich experience of priceless value in the church. Still he retains the same childish spirit with all its genial, joyous vivacity, which once made him loved at first sight as the boy-preacher by a generation that is gradually passing away.

We have spoken of "*the Church*" as if it were a corporate body in its articles of fellowship and government "*independent*" of other churches and equally independent of "*the ruling Elder,*" elected for the time being to fill the pulpit and to fulfill the functions of pastor. This however is a mere fiction, the church-books notwithstanding. To the apprehension of every member, "*the Church at the Metropolitan Tabernacle*" as a living organization, is and always has been a company of Christ's disciples, over which Mr. Spurgeon takes the oversight. Definitions are seldom or ever very trustworthy and popular convictions are generally more reliable than private explanations. "One flock and one Shepherd" may suffice to describe the true church of the living God, so far as it is at present manifested. The Shepherd's voice is the bond of their fellowship; the sheep of his pasture know his voice and they follow him. In like manner the communities gathered as "Christian churches" are best distinguished by their ministers. This is so obviously a fact in our experience that we may as well acknowledge it, to whatever censure it may expose us. Not one of the seven churches of Asia was more closely identified with the angel of that church than is the Tabernacle-church with its pastor. With gratitude which lips cannot tell nor language record, we regard Mr. Spurgeon as *a star* in the right hand of him who walked in the midst of the golden candlesticks; a star that has reflected light on many lands; a preacher whose voice has gone forth to the ends of the earth; but to many of us "a father in Christ Jesus," whose tender solicitude for our welfare has helped our faith, hallowed our homes and guided our marches through twenty-five years of our earthly pilgrimage.

The oak is scarcely more unlike the acorn from which it sprung than is the Metropolitan Tabernacle of to-day to the New Park Street Chapel of twenty-five years ago. The present church, however, with its muster-roll of five thousand members, its deeply rooted sympathies and its widely spread branches, has sprung up and developed from the little fellowship of the past by a natural growth. Nothing strange or miraculous has happened at any time, and yet by constant increase month after month a result has accumulated which by its greatness excites our gratitude. A continual providence, rather than a conspicuous prodigy, leads us to exclaim, "What hath God wrought!" Mr. Spurgeon never seemed to have plan or project, purpose or proposal that foreshadowed the stupendous constitution over which he now presides. But he always watched the course of events and never to our knowledge lost an opportunity of extending the sphere of his labours. Thus he began his career in London by preaching whenever he had a chance of telling the old tale to a new audience, and wherever he saw "an open door."

It was rather startling to hear him read on a Sunday evening the catalogue of his engagement for the week. Finding then how sinners were converted, backsliders reclaimed, and believers refreshed by his sermons, he began to fancy he had slightly mistaken his vocation, and earnestly doubted whether he ought not rather to go forth as an evangelist, than to maintain his status as pastor, merely taking the oversight of one flock. Special providences in connection with the purchase of a freehold site, and the rearing of an edifice so suitable, that it seemed as if the finger of God directed architect, builder, and artisans, speedily resolved his scruples, and he was led clearly to discern how he could magnify his office as a pastor while he pursued the work of an evangelist. Had he not acted in the double capacity, the funds would not have been forthcoming to open our colossal sanctuary free of debt. The provinces of all England paid their quota in response to his mission services, and in almost every instance the county churches were enriched by their contributions, as he rarely received more than the moiety of the sums voluntarily subscribed at his visits.

From the earliest outset of his ministry among us Mr. Spurgeon showed a love of work, a capacity for work, and a zeal for one particular work which he accounted it the object of his life to carry forward. His master-purpose has always been to diffuse the knowledge of the Gospel. The noviciates he drew round him were almost to a man enamored of his enthusiasm and anxious to emulate it. Young men went out of New Park Street Chapel, and Exeter Hall, to preach themselves at the street corners. In some instances their zeal outran their discretion. The increasing number of candidates for church fellowship raised the question how each one was to be attended to, the sincerity of his profession judiciously weighed, strict inquiry into moral character be invariably made and a regular supervision maintained over all who were baptized and enrolled on the church-books. After much prayer and deliberation, Mr. Spurgeon saw his way to the revival of the office of "*Elder*," which had fallen into desuetude, at least in our churches. Very modestly he suggested this method to meet an exigence sorely felt: but very palpably, with some deviations from the plan then inaugurated, has it received tokens of divine sanction and blessing. The Elders in our midst are all men of exemplary piety, who consecrate as much time and talent as they can call their own to seeking the welfare of the people. Most of them have individually found some special sphere of service to which they are ardently attached: while all of them in concert devote themselves to seeking out anxious inquirers, visiting the sick and sorrowing, and attending to unhappy cases in which serious defections on the part of members call for the solemn discipline of the church.

Our Elders, who are chosen rather by recognition of their character and their service than by any haphazard estimate of their suitability, are annually elected and re-elected to their office: their present labours of love being their qualification. There never has been a dissentient voice at any nomination: or has there been at any time a difficulty in dropping the name from the list of honourable officers when from any cause whatever any one has ceased to be profitable to the church. The grace of God and the guidance of the Holy Spirit have been remarkably exemplified in the wisdom and prudence of these "Elders." The young men and young women who have devoted themselves to the Sunday Schools, the tract-distribution and visiting societies and the town and country local preaching associations have been for the most part approved, trained, and superintended by one or other of these distinguished brethren. Their praise can never be fully told. To a gracious influence and not to a worldly affluence we must trace the readiness of men who have their livelihood to earn by their labours to consecrate every hour of their leisure and every ounce of their strength to do what just lay before them for the love of Christ and the welfare of his people.

As for the Deacons, had it not been for a succession of able men, with willing hearts and open hands, a sound knowledge of things secular, and a sincere appreciation of things spiritual, it is hard to see how such a host of enterprises as were successively undertaken, could have been effectually carried out. Many of these enterprises have their local habitation, and their visible monuments as well as their distinct and enduring name. They represent real invested capital and show a large annual balance sheet. The College-buildings, the Orphanage for fatherless boys, and the Almshouses severally stand on freehold sites, and have each a substantial foundation which far as human prescience can descry, will save them from the sneers of satirists in days to come. We think they have not grown up like gourds or multiplied like mushrooms, with the like proclivity to perish. How much of Mr. Spurgeon's scrupulous caution is due to those comic detractors, who were wont to pose him persistently with problems as to what would come of the Tabernacle, if he should chance to die, we cannot tell: but sure we are that in all his schemes he has been shrewd enough to secure the solvency of his survivors.

"THE PASTORS' COLLEGE LOAN BUILDING AND RESERVE FUND," by its advances has helped to rear many a sanctuary in all parts of the country. Liberal contributions provided the fund which gives the donors a large interest in the welfare of many little churches. Mr. Spurgeon's personal devotedness has drawn around him *Deacons* who have done their duty. Of the brethren who held the office a quarter of a century ago, not one remains: they have all fallen asleep. They were venerable men when he was a stripling: and ripe to retire when he buckled on the harness. With one exception they were then past the time of life when fresh adventures commend themselves to the judgement. They no longer had the vigour and enthusiasm requisite to make success a certainty. That they had already served their generation faithfully the church-records fully prove. Still Mr. Spurgeon saw the necessity of planning his own campaigns; so he blew the trumpet, gathered round him fresh recruits, and selected his own officers, while he assailed the indifference and infidelity, which he found rife in the metropolis and the provinces.

Father Olney lived long enough to hail the new and brighter era. For many years, the dear old gentleman accompanied the young preacher in most of his public engagements, taking a seat by his side in the pulpit or on the platform, both in town and country, as his silent but constant friend. Well did he merit the title of "*the good deacon*." His sons abide with us, worthy successors of such a sire. During the past quarter of a century, valuable officers have come and gone, shedding a sweet savour for a short season. Some of the present deacons were members of the church before Mr. Spurgeon began his pastorate; others have been members almost from the beginning: but though the junior in years he is officially the senior of the group.

Never during the twenty-five years we have under review was the work greater, the responsibility heavier or the harmony purer than at present. Willing hands always wanted where there is so much work to be done, but we see fresh contingents constantly coming to the front. Moreover, joyfully we hail them. For we are bound to recognise good men as God's choicest gifts to the church, even as the God-man, our Lord Jesus Christ, must ever be regarded as His unspeakable gift. Should the history of the church at the Tabernacle ever be written in the time to come by one to whom the pure facts come filtered from all paltry details, it will be worthy of mention that the highest in office was the lowliest in drudgery; that the dominant counsellor was literally the chief doorkeeper; that the wealthiest benefactors kept themselves in the background; and that the Pastor's intimate friends and coadjutors never sought any prominence: for while he himself conscientiously ignored all self-interest, it was absolutely essential that those who worked with him should seek, not their own, but the things of Jesus Christ.

Among the ministries of love which have arisen in the church to aid the Pastor, and to advance the cause of true religion, *that* of devout women has never been wanting among us. To the piety of our sisters, we owe some the choicest flowers and ripest fruits of a living faith. The influence they shed is often silent as the dew; but good deeds publish their own praise by the lips of those who partake of the benefit. Thus, it was with Mrs. Bartlett's class for young women. It grew and kept on growing so steadily that it became a marvel for its magnitude, and made her name familiar. While she lived, she continued to be a winner of souls, and when she died, she left fragrant memories behind, for her good conversation was an ornament to *our* profession.

And thus, it is with *Mrs. Spurgeon's Book Fund*, which has opened a new mine of sympathy, and provided a fresh outlet for benevolence, by supplying the Levites of our land with gospel literature. As God gives special grace for special service, so this suffering saint has enabled to enrich the libraries of poor pastors with grants of books, thus helping those who sow the good seed of the kingdom by putting a little more corn into their baskets. During the past three years, our pastor's wife has distributed nearly twenty thousand volumes, having collected and expended more than three thousand five hundred pounds, while Presbyterian and Episcopalian, Methodist and Congregational ministers have participated with Baptists in the bounty.

The Monday Evening Prayer Meeting has been the principal means of promoting and maintaining the spiritual vitality of the church. To it, we owe incidentally an acquaintance with one another, an appreciation of each other's gifts, and a care for each other's welfare. From it, we have gained a frequent recurrence of revivals, and by it, we have secured a unity of heart amidst a variety of operations. To a comparatively select audience Mr. Spurgeon has preached on Sunday mornings: on the Sabbath evenings, a promiscuous multitude has hung on his lips: but on Monday evenings, we have seen and known and felt his pastoral influence.

To maintain freshness and force in his devotional exercises over taxes the faculties of many a minster. We have sometimes heard of those who yearned for a liturgy to afford them some relief. However, the strain of leading a band of suppliants and keeping up the fervour of the services week by week, year after year, is obviously far more severe. Doubtless, it is a labour of love, yet the assiduity of our pastor in feeding the fire and fanning the flames of devotion among the *members*, and especially among the *workers* of the church has been unflagging and exemplary. Regular and punctual in his own attendance, he has instilled a zest into the hearts of his fellow-worshippers. At this gathering of the fraternity, he has been wont to pour out his soul before God with peculiar freedom. It has been likewise his habit to intersperse short addresses, in which with simple ingenuousness he has unfolded the secret workings of his own mind, the anxieties he felt, or the hopes he cherished: and when sympathies have been sufficiently kindled, some trusty bother has been called upon to lead the supplication, or give vent to the thanksgiving of the assembling.

In this manner he has encouraged all his fellow-labourers to unburden themselves of every apprehension and disquietude at the mercy-seat, and to resort thither for strength and guidance. And, by these means he has succeeded in gauging the sympathies of the community. The fellowship enjoyed in these privileged hours has thus proved a faithful index to the ebb and flow of church life in our midst. Those members of the church who do not habitually frequent our prayer-meetings know little of the latent springs that have fed the tide of her prosperity, and they have failed to participate in the joy of such times of refreshing as no tongue can describe. So much of communion with the Lord has proved. So often those who have come to the assembly with sad faces, in deep straits, have gone away after a concert of prayer with their dark forebodings dissipated, their courage quickened, their course made plain, and their countenance no more sad. So frequently has the power of the Holy Spirit been felt in causing us to be of one accord, till in pains and pleasures we have had unison of heart in our supplications, which lay open or led up to a unanimity of purpose that no mutual explanations or multiplicity of arguments could have equally secured.

In such primitive fashion, our harmony has been preserved because it has never been hazarded. Love has made labour light, and we have found that grievances never grate or canker when we take them to the mercy seat. Of those who stand aloof from the inner circle of our fellowship, some whose occupations hinder them subscribe to our enterprises the more freely because they can engage so little in personal service. In a working church, however, the co-operation of all the members is welcome. If any continue not with us in our labours of love, their counsels are never sought, their cautions are never heeded, and their criticisms are never valued. They can only count for cyphers in the congregation. There is a niche for each individual to fill, did he only know where to find it. The pastor is always on the lookout to select a post for a person, or a person for a post; and it invariably proves much to our friends' comfort, and much more to the church's compactness, if in every instance some appropriate sphere occupied.

Our ancient church has a modern history which at this passing hour we are mainly intent to celebrate. A fresh point of departure was signalised by the opening of the Metropolitan Tabernacle in the month of March, 1861. Those who followed the camp during the nomad period when our Sabbath assemblies were held at times in the west and at other times in the south of London will revoke with lively interest the epoch of our entrance into the new edifice. With a flush of real joy, and with a ring of hearty cheers, the announcement was hailed that the home in which we were assembled was our own freehold, unencumbered with debt. Let our thanksgivings to God be offered afresh today as we remember it. Perhaps future generations will rehearse the strain: it is meet they should, for his mercy endured forever.

The pastor was a little impatient of the inaugural meetings. He would not have it presumed that we had entered into rest, when we merely halted on our forward march. The logic of his reasoning is worthy of permanent record. He argued that as we had experienced so many providential helps while we were in sore straits, it was hardly desirable ever to wish for a smooth passage. He estimated the moral responsibilities of the church with a keen appreciation of what might reasonably be expected of her by neighbours on all sides; and with a strong conviction that no good would come of so large a concourse of people, unless greater works were done to the glory of God. Knowing his own popularity, he feared lest the Tabernacle should become a mere preaching station. The wide range of his sympathies and the close scrutiny of his conscience pointed his own course; but it was all a question then who would follow his lead. He saw that a prodigious body would become unwieldy if it were not well-proportioned; and to his apprehension, the church would become isolated if the members were indolent. As he looked at the rising aggregation of members, he saw that it would be a strange anomaly if there were not a proportionate accession of strength. Fidelity alone can save us from failure, was his warning note, for we have before us a grand opportunity, and to miss it can be nothing less than a glaring folly. With prayers as memorable as his preaching he entreated the Lord while he exhorted the people. The methods he used challenge notice, not so much for their novelty as for their combining two courses of action that are often the marks of wide divergence. In starting each enterprise he took the whole responsibility; but in maturing it he was never jealous of taking all the credit to himself.

It was always with him a matter of principle to rear all sacred institutions in the garden of the church; but he has shown a scrupulous anxiety to prove their vitality before he put them in such a conspicuous place. As the acorns and the pips from which oak and apple trees grow are first planted in flower-pots and only transplanted into fields and orchards when they have fairly sprouted and given some indications of vigour, so Mr. Spurgeon has privately tended every project on the outset. No committee did he ever form till he had some promising plant to commit to their custody.

THE PASTORS' COLLEGE is regarded by many Christian friends who do not belong to our fellowship as a singular phenomenon. Their surprise would be greater if they knew the artless simplicity with which it was originally started and the singular God-speed with which it has developed.

In the past generations our baptized churches used to send out pastors when they judged them to have sacred gifts and a divine call to the ministry. Pious youths were sometimes boarded with ministers of repute, by whom they were educated and trained. The old plan was superseded by colleges founded with devout convictions, and supported with pious intentions. This modern proceeding, however, did not appear to be free from some rather formidable objections. More than one principal had lamented the spiritual deterioration of his pupils while they passed through their course of studies. The complaint was that "the young men who came in with hearts on fire and empty heads went out with heads full of learning but with frozen hearts." "We had better [return] to some of our old habits," said the young minister of New Park Street Chapel; and forthwith he arranged to pay out of his own purse for the education of one youth at the house of a Baptist minister. Not long afterwards he met on a public platform the pastor of a small country church who seemed to him endowed with talents, but sorely trammeled for want of education. A generous offer to pay for his taking a course of lessons was gratefully accepted, with a result that secured many benefits to the obliged and very much pleasure to the benefactor.

The Pastors' College was unconsciously projected, when the pastor took a few friends into his confidence and obtained a short list of subscribers to the obligations he was gradually incurring: though it was not formally realized till after the Tabernacle was reared. Six or seven students had already become pensioners on his thrifty bond, when he took an opportunity at the weekly prayer-meeting of calling upon two of them to lead the devotions, and of explaining at the same time the plan he was pursuing. From that hour the church felt a lively interest in the work. A few members took it up with enthusiasm; others followed in the wake, until at length it became a constituent part of our church organization. We need hardly apologize for naming Mr. William Olney, as the earliest contributor when the College was in embryo; Mr. J. R. Phillips, whose generous gift of an annual supper had made it familiar to thousands of his guests; or Mr. W. C. Murrell, who by initiating and superintending the Weekly Offering has secured the co-operation not of members only, but of visitors to the Tabernacle in aid of its support.

For upwards of twelve years the students met in the lecture-hall and class-rooms, at the basement of the Tabernacle. Not till the number of these probationers had so multiplied that it became alike unhealthy and inconvenient to assemble in such straitened quarters, was a vigorous effort made to secure a site in close proximity and to build an edifice suited to their requirements. Mr. Spurgeon enlisted sympathy enough to justify his initiating the movement. When the parish church of St. Mary, Newington, was removed an eligible plot in the rear of the Tabernacle was obtained. We all recognized in this a kindly providence. After the principal part of the capital had been found, a considerable balance was required to clear off the cost.

On a day not soon to be forgotten the beloved pastor gave a day's attendance to receive the votive offerings of willing subscribers. The members came in one continuous stream to testify their gratitude to God for the good they had derived from his ministry, everyone with a gift in hand, and yet more generous each than any gratuity could express. There was no spirit of grudging in the small benefactions: the poorer the man the more he appreciated the privilege of becoming a partner in the good work. Trustees were not nominated till the president could say, "I have invested enough to protect you from liabilities for keeping it in good order. If I die, I desire that no one of you should have to encounter a demand through the recklessness of my adventures."

Fresh concords have been promoted in the fellowship of our church by enlarging the field of her enterprise. Conspicuous among her charities is THE ORPHANAGE FOR FATHERLESS BOYS. Though situated at Stockwell, about two miles south of the Tabernacle, it virtually rests under her shadow. Mrs. Hillyard's generous proposal in the autumn of 1866 to consecrate twenty thousand pounds towards founding such an institution was the earliest foreshadow of the present noble asylum. When Mr. Spurgeon was asked to accept this offering in trust, his ingenuous character, and his administrative abilities, rather than any partiality to the section of Protestants he was identified with, guided the lady in selecting him as the trustee of her bounty. Under his supervision the original scheme was greatly enlarged. Following the dictates of his conscience, with a kind of instinct, he appealed to the church. There are other associations for praiseworthy objects, but the church is the only sacred society under the immediate sanction of our Lord Jesus Christ. His policy prospered. Mrs. Hillyard's principal was not tampered with; it was not even touched. The freehold site was purchased by subscriptions: the separate houses were reared, as their various designations indicate, by the free gifts of individuals or of societies.

A remarkable spontaneousness made it evident that the opportunity was hailed of paying a grateful tribute to Mr. Spurgeon for the services he had rendered to several departments of the church, and very notably to the whole denomination of Baptists. Fifty lads were at first taken in charge; and while that number has been gradually increased fivefold, bequests unfettered by any condition have enabled the trustees to double the invested capital. Towards the current expenditure there has been a steady and constant inflow, generally sufficient for the day, occasionally supplemented by larger gifts, which have relieved the executive from anxiety. The deacons of the church are, for the most part, the Trustees of the Orphanage. Our faith in the Father of the fatherless has been thus far amply rewarded, though sometimes slightly tried. On one occasion when the funds ran low, the president cast five hundred pounds into the treasury to meet the ordinary outlay his interest in this, as in all other departments of which he takes the oversight, being never honour without onus. By a kindly providence, however, the supplies have generally been plentiful.

The whole aim, however, is not compassed by housing, feeding, and clothing these poor lads. A primary object is to train them as a Christian family in the fear of the Lord: and we have good reason to believe that the master, and each of the matrons, watches for their souls. Bitter would have been the disappointment had none of them become disciples of Christ. On the contrary, it is gratifying to know that many have received the good seed of gospel into their hearts before they have gone forth to take part in the industries of life. Some few have died in the faith, very happy, and fully assured that they were going to be with Jesus. The testimony that several of these little ones left behind was truly refreshing. One pupil, after passing through the College, has entered the ministry; another is now a student in the Pastor's College; and a third holds office as a junior teacher in the Orphanage. Music has been cultivated among the boys with much success, and a choir of considerable efficiency has been formed. Under Mr. Vernon Charlesworth's able leadership a band of forty or fifty boys has performed a sacred concert in various provincial towns. By the invitations they receive, the welcome that is given them and the satisfaction expressed with their conduct, it is evident that the institution is becoming year by year more widely known and more highly appreciated.

In what secret chamber THE TABERNACLE COLPORTAGE ASSOCIATION took its rise we do not know, but its earliest recognition we well remember. It was at a prayer-meeting in the autumn of 1866. Many even of our younger members must recollect the circumstances. There was something humorous in the manner in which the first contingent came to the front. After the Pastor's wont, he gave a broad description of the work itself and of the wayfarers engaged in it. Two or three of these trusty travellers held themselves in readiness to tell the tale of their travels, while one of them was talking about his pack; Mr. Spurgeon called on him to strap it on his back. He did so, and in full working costume finished his speech, amidst cheers so loud, that he was at once chosen as a *model of the order*, and his photograph has grown familiar, as it graces all our Reports. The enthusiasm awakened at that meeting has been revived again and again at every fresh gathering of the clan. A genial disposition and a spice of mother-wit must be combined with a devout character and a busy-bee-like diligence to qualify any man for an office in which there is such a blend of the laborious trade of a hawker with the lofty profession of an evangelist. But we can bear our men witness that they do the drudgery of the one and bear the dignity of the other without being distracted by either. Their vocation lies beyond the pale of our ordinary pastorates; so we have much to learn as we listen to their addresses. The colloquies they hold as pedlars with some of our country cousins often sound very droll, and the illustrations they use when preaching in rural districts occasionally seem to us rather quaint.

As the Hebrew patriarchs reared altars to the Lord their God of the unhewn stones they found in the neighbourhood, so gospel sermons addressed to rustic swains gain point and piquancy from the unpolished phrases picked up among the locals. Our colporteurs are sound in the faith. They feed the people with true manner, and if they do borrow the dishes in which it is served up from the villagers, it may fairly excite a smile, though it will barely excuse a sneer. Vulgarity is the vice commonly charged upon the teachers who go forth from the Tabernacle. We have no wish to complain of the imputation, but we should like to explain our own position in respect to it. There are two kinds of vulgarity. The one sort debases the well-bred with its profanities, while the other sort abases the scholar with its simplicities. We have no taste for the attic salt that draws ribald jests out of Holy Scriptures, but we have a pure relish for the genius that can translate the tales and the teaching of our Saxon Bibles into the homespun dialects of our unlettered hamlets.

Our mission, in all its various agencies, is to the masses of the people in populous cities, expanding towns, and neglected villages, and our success hinges on our sympathies. The agricultural population of this county reflects little credit on the proprietors of the land. Till an "Arch" bishop outside the ecclesiastical establishment was raised up to rouse the peasants to assert their rights, they were like serfs in dreary servility, knit to the soil, and held in mental moral bondage by parson and squire. Happily their emancipation is now in their own hands and the light of heaven will lead them to a heritage of liberty.

Meanwhile we can afford to smile at the reproaches of those clever men who indulge in theological speculations without any religious convictions. We cannot hope to please those dainty critics of whom it has been truly said that they are more familiar with the classics than the

Scriptures, which they know more of the labours of Hercules than of the sufferings of Jesus, and that they are better acquainted with Olympus and Parnassus than they are with Sinai and Calvary. Their taste can never supply a rule for our testimony. What could be paltry on our part than to parley with connoisseurs when we have a contract on hand with but a short space of time to perform it? Our policy is to avail ourselves of any faithful labourers, be they skilled or unskilled. Howbeit, all our labourers are learners and they will all grow proficient by degrees, if only they persevere, each one in his calling.

In the matter of ways and means we are supposed to be open to abundant congratulation, and we must admit that we have cause for abounding gratitude. By an opportune Providence our needs have been always supplied and we have lacked nothing. But let not any man think that in waiting upon God there is no trial of faith. To be brought low and then to be helped gives a sharp spur to gratitude. Full often have we feared that we were rather floundering than flourishing. "*He that is ready to slip with his feet,*" said an old patriarch, "*is as a lamp despised in the thought of him that is at ease.*" The great lamps that light the pilgrim through the world are men whose principles have shone through mists and fogs, when neither sun nor stars appeared for many a day. And the bright and shining light that illuminates the Metropolitan Tabernacle, sending forth clear beams visible in distant lands, forms no exception to the inspired rule. We are witnesses of the painful solicitudes he often endured before the welcome succour came, and the miseries that haunted his imagination on the very eve of those halcyon days of mercy that the Lord has vouchsafed to cheer him. The incessant watchfulness requisite for so vast an oversight as he exercises has never permitted him to be long at ease, for seldom has a great deliverance sprung up in one quarter than a rude alarm of anger has suddenly arisen in another.

Mr. Spurgeon's trust in God has never prompted him to relax his own toil. On the other hand it has made him redouble his exertions so many times, that we stand aghast at the multiplicity of his labours. He wants more pocket-money for extra expenses and casual outlays than any man we ever heard of. A great portion of this God grants him by blessing the labour of his hands and the fruitfulness of his brains, and then donations are also put into his hands to meet contingencies for which none of the special gifts for specific objects would be available. Though he never pretended to be a priest, devout thank-offerings, peace-offerings, and free-will offerings are thus often privately committed to his keeping, to be distributed in the Lord's service according to his judgment.

By the issue of his monthly serial, *"The Sword and the Trowel,"* he keeps up a correspondence with his many friends and helpers. The magazine circulates on its own merits, supplying subscribers with devout literature. In this periodical the editor's pen is conspicuous: and it has answered many useful purposes. Contributors to our various institutions obtain in its columns an acknowledgment of their benefactions, and a large constituency is kept well informed of all that is going on in the "Notes." The workers in our own hive either tell their own tale, or a better description than they supply is graphically related by a special reporter: and the workers in other hives are remembered in its columns. The biographies of Christian men who have served their generation well are epitomized. And indeed so substantial is the provision of the magazine that several volumes have been constructed out of reprints of its articles. Notably was this the case with "John Ploughman's Talk." And the series of Expositions of the Psalms since published under the title of *"The Treasury of David"* was commenced in the early numbers of *"The Sword and the Trowel."*

It will be readily conceded that Mr. Spurgeon has developed far more talent of his own than he was conscious of himself when he began his ministry. But in the process of unravelling his own capacities he has learnt to believe in the aptitudes of other people. Starting with the stern Calvinistic doctrine that there is no good quality in the creature, so utterly corrupt and ruined is man by the fall, he has gradually proceeded to make it plain and proven that there is no good of which he is not capable, if only the heart be renewed by grace. Not a few individuals who seemed to themselves but dry sticks has he been the means of grafting into the vine so effectually that to their own astonishment, they have become branches bearing much fruit. With habitual modesty he constantly attributes to Sunday-school teachers, tract distributors, and in fact to the entire rank and file of Christian workers, the real praise for results of which he gets all the credit. This is true in a degree, although it is even truer that his accomplished generalship made the soldiers. It is difficult to imagine any other leader that could have fashioned such efficient instruments out of the same material.

A resolution to celebrate THE SILVER WEDDING of the pastor with the church was at once cordially adopted and has been successfully carried out. By these presents, we thank God; no chapter of our history is closed. The work of the house of the Lord is in full progress. Behold the pastor! His youth is renewed like the eagle's. In the midst of the years he has had an interval to meditate. And as a giant refreshed he has returned to the fray. Behold the pastor's sons! How full of promise they look now that they have just buckled on their armour, and stand waiting for their station. See the machinery of our church organization! Is there a speck of rust on the wheels or cogs? We hope not. Behold the Pastors' College! Is it not breaking up fresh ground, and sending forth missionaries to the far-off lands with many a prayer and aspiration that brighter days may soon dawn on the heathen world? Behold the Orphanage! It is only beginning to yield its first fruits to the fellowship of the church. As for our Evangelistic and Colporteur Associations, they seem to have merely made such trial trips as have proved their sea-worthiness; and we look forward to their carrying large freights of precious souls on the heavenly voyage. We greet on all sides the awakening influence of spring; but our strength is in God, and from him our expectation cometh. By the conscious presence of the Lord Jesus Christ in our midst and the continual renewing of the Holy Ghost, the blessed toils of pastor and people may yet prosper more abundantly in the future than they have done in the past.

COMMENTS AFTER THE PAPER

Mr. SPURGEON said: I take it as a great act of self-denying affection on the part of Mr. Carr that he has left out in the reading so much of what he had carefully prepared. It has always been a singular feature with my friends here that if they work hard and prepare a paper or a speech they are quite content to leave out even the best parts of it, or to remain silent altogether, if it seems wisest to do so: this I regard as one of the highest tests of discipline and surest proofs of love. In this, which some may count a small thing; I see the strength of the attachment which exists between us. No one among you gives me offence, or takes offence at what I do. I can never understand all this love, nor why it gathers around me. I can only use over again the simile I have employed before. In the crystallizing of sugar, to make sugar candy, strings are stretched across the vessel in which the syrup is boiled; upon these strings the sugar crystallizes. I am one of those strings. You are the sugar, the divine life supplies the fire which prepares your hearts and I am the thread around which you crystallize. So be it still. You will have Mr. Carr's admirable paper in full when it is printed and you will not forget with what perfect acquiescence and hearty cheerfulness he shortened it in the public reading, lest there should be an approach to weariness on your part. Never leader had such officers or soldiers either.

The anthem, "Cry out and shout" was then sung, after which Mr. Spurgeon said: "Perhaps, dear friends, it would be well to have just a little interval between the papers. I have been informed that our friend Mr. Wigner comes here on an errand which he will probably be glad to discharge at once."

PASTOR J. T. WIGNER, who was accompanied by Mr. William Higgs, then came forward, and said, "My dear Mr. Spurgeon and my Christian friends, My dear friend Mr. Higgs and myself are here this evening as a deputation from the committee of the London Baptist association, and I feel it an unspeakable honour and privilege to be permitted to bring a letter from the committee of that association to read to this assembly tonight and to present to our beloved and honored brother, Mr. Spurgeon, on the occasion of his pastoral 'silver wedding.' I shall not detain you five minutes, but will read the letter, and leave it to tell its own tale."

The following letter was then read by the Speaker: "To the Rev. C. H. Spurgeon.

"Dear Friend and Brother, The Committee of the London Baptist Association cannot deny themselves the pleasure of adding their congratulations to the many which will be offered to you on the present auspicious occasion. We do this on behalf of the one hundred and fifty churches in the Association, and we have requested our brethren, J. T Wigner and W. Higgs to express our feelings by word of mouth. Next to your own church, we venture to claim an interest in your continued health and ability for labour. We recognize in you one of the honored fathers and founders of our Association. We rejoice in your long and abundant career of usefulness. We join our thanksgivings and prayers with those of the whole Church of Christ on your behalf. May you be long spared to preach the gospel which you love so much and to be the leader in the manifold Christian agencies which you have so successfully originated, and in every season of weakness and depression may you be comforted with those consolations which you have learned so well to administer to others. We desire to express also our hearty congratulations to the church at the Tabernacle, with its elders and deacons, and to your loved brother and colleague in the pastorate. Our Association is always made to feel itself at home at the Tabernacle, and we earnestly invoke upon its entire brotherhood the blessing of the great Head of the Church, our common Lord and Savior."

On behalf of the Committee, Yours faithfully and affectionately,

William Brock, Vice-President

Mount Grove, Hampstead, May 20, 1879.

MR. WIGNER added (turning to the chairman): Dear Mr. Spurgeon, it affords me ever great pleasure to pass that letter to you as a feeble expression of the love we bear you, of the heartfelt gratitude we feel today that you are so far restored, and in the midst of your people again. We adore the mercy of God that he has brought you back. We thought of you, and we prayed for you in your absence; and we bless God that our prayers have been heard. If I might venture on behalf of the brethren to make one remark, I would say, do not accept a solitary invitation to preach anywhere besides the Tabernacle for at least twelve months to come not because, my dear brother, we should not all value your services and heartily welcome you, but we want, by God's mercy, to see you fully and permanently restored, and we feel that at present the work of this vast church and its agencies is enough to tax your strength to the very uttermost. We thank God on your behalf. We thank God on your behalf for your beloved sons rising up into the ministry, and we pray that they may be with you, very successful labourers in the work of God. But do, pray, keep at home! And if any church, or any pastor, or any association between this and the 20th of May, 1880, shall ask you to preach, say in unmistakable terms, "I won't!"

Mr. SPURGEON: All of which is exceedingly good advice. At the same time, it is impossible to carry it out; there are so many things that *must be* done. I thank the Association heartily, and wish prosperity to all its churches. Now, if you had heard Mr. Carr's paper all through it would have made it, I think, even more apparent than you have already seen, that whilst God has been doing a very great work in our midst, and not in our midst only, but a work spreading abroad from us in all sorts of ways, yet it has not been my work. I said last night, as plainly and distinctly as I could put it into human words, that I have been only the outward and visible sign of the inward and spiritual grace working behind in many other hearts. I told the friends last night some incidents which would illustrate this. I want to mention one now, and that is that as to the oversight of the church, the meetings with the elders, the looking after the cases of discipline, and other matters of pastoral work, if these be well done the gratitude is due to those elders who do the work, and at their head to my brother, who behind the scenes, and unobserved by the most of you, is working hard. If you were to observe him becoming very prominent in that matter it would seem as if a great many of you had to be looked after. We want that work to be as much unseen as possible; but it is none the less needful, and none the less difficult, and none the less does it require divine guidance. It is well also to mark how my brother performs the very difficult task of being second man. Almost any fool can go first, but it takes an uncommonly wise man to go second. I recall what he said when he first came among us, that if two men rode a horse one would have to ride behind; and he promised that I should ride in front and he would sit behind *and hold me on*. I always liked the idea, and I think he has thoroughly carried it out.

I should not like the papers to be read by anyone without a distinct recognition that anything said about me is not about me; I am merely the representative of the whole lot of you, my brother, the deacons, the elders, and the whole church. And then I should not like what is said about this one church to seem as if it were said about us as an isolated community, but about a part of the body of Jesus Christ, in which the Holy Spirit works most graciously. If I said that it has not been a great and wonderful work I should lie before God and my own conscience, but if in the remotest degree I should appear to take any shade of credit to myself I should be equally false to my own conscience and to my God. I do not know whether my brother would like to say anything to you, but he has all the time before him for the next few minutes. For me it must suffice to say that I love and admire him not only as my brother after the flesh, but as my faithful fellow-helper in the pastorate of this church and in all else of our common service.

PASTOR J. A. SPURGEON said: My dear Christian friends, I am quite out of place here in the front, because you know that whilst my brother is in the chair I really never have any work to do; it is only when he does not happen to be here that my true position appears. I think I had better keep that seat behind, of which you have heard; that is the happiest place, I find. My brother says that any fool can lead, but I say that any fool can follow. When my brother in front goes ahead and does the work it is very easy for me to come behind and tread in his steps. I do thank God, however, if I have been able to spare my brother, and I think I have, some of the drudgery of the work. That I deem an honour which any man might covet; and I esteem it to be the crowning honour of the work which God had laid upon me. I only hope that I shall be spared for many years to continue to help him and the less I have to do in this respect the better, because that means that my brother has strength and health to do it himself. I can remember him longer than any one of you, I have received more from him than any one of you; I only shine with a borrowed light, and I have to thank God for more than twenty-five years in which he has been my teacher and my guide in spiritual things. Well, now, I expect to meet a great many of you at the jubilee. I do not see any reason why not. At the beginning of the twenty-five years now closed, we were just as likely to be here as we are likely to be there, speaking after the manner of men. I hope my brother has got the twenty-five better years still in store. I distinctly remember my grandfather at eighty-two rubbing his knees and saying that the gout would shorten his days. I hope I shall see my good brother rubbing his knees at eighty-two, and longer still if God shall will it. Long may we be spared to work together as we have done in the past, serving the Lord our God.

I have been asked many, many times, "What is the secret of the great success at the Tabernacle?" I do not think I could ever give a better answer than that which I once gave to one of the most unlikely people in the world to ask the question. I went into a Jew's shop at the Shoreditch to purchase something, and when the man there found out that my name was Spurgeon, he wanted to know whether I was related to the great man of that name. When I told him that I had the honour to be his brother, he shut the door, looked all-round the shop to see that no one was listening, and then asked me, "What is the secret of his great success?" I said, "I think it lies in the fact that he loves Jesus of Nazareth, and Jesus of Nazareth loves him." I said "I do not mean to put that offensively to you, knowing what you are, but I do believe that in those two facts, you will find the secret of his success." It is my brother's immense love to his Master, and it is the Master's infinite love to him, that is the secret of our great gathering here to-night.

9. "The Baptist Churches: Twenty-Five Years Ago and Now"

By Rev. C. Stanford, D.D., May 20, 1879 (*MV*)

AFTER the grip and the glow of words about your own particular home, and the strings of delight with which you have heard your own particular story, all that I have to say about the story of the other Baptist churches during the same period of twenty-five years will naturally sound like tame talk about things in general. Yet, if you can, hear me. Hear me first speak for a moment or two about that much calumniated word "Baptist," into which it is thought by some that the soul of our denomination is cramped and shut up like a lovely plant in a tight pot. The gentlemen who think so have not the pleasure of knowing us.

Cut with knife or nail in the wall of the old prison chamber at Lambeth Palace, unknown centuries ago, I find in Latin this inscription:—"Jesus is my Love", reminding me of the sentence ascribed to Ignatius, "My Love is crucified." What confessor wrote these words upon the wall? Perhaps he was a Baptist Lollard, perhaps a seminary priest; but no man can infer what his denomination was from the fact of his loyalty to Jesus. This I know, Baptist or no Baptist, sure as he had this loyalty, and sure as I have I belong to that man and that man belongs to me, "world without end, amen." But as of old, "a man of Benjamin, a mighty man of valour" did not the less belong to his own little tribe because he belonged to the commonwealth of Israel; so now a man need not be the less a Baptist because he glories in the essential oneness of himself with all believers. "Your distinctive tenet," say some, "is a little thing to make the standard of a tribe." We repudiate that imputation of littleness. If we are wrong in our reading of what Christ commands as the initial act of our Christian profession, the meaning of that act is not little, the consequences of it are not little, and the principle of obedience is not little; we therefore say to our courteous critics, one and all, "we naturally want to know how our own tribe gets on in the world, for it would be bad for us, bad for you, and bad for the whole world, if Baptists were to go down."

I. In glancing at the history of the last twenty-five years, first, I have to report *some of our encouragements*. One of these is *numerical increase*. Leaving for the present all measurement of our progress with the ratio of progress in the national population; not even daring to look at the grand field of our foreign mission, nor indeed at any of our mission fields; not appropriating the countless casuals and ecclesiastical irregulars who hold our baptismal tenet, but who are not to be found in our congregations; and simply drawing information from our institutional books and papers, allow me to offer, for what they are worth, these few comparative sum totals:

Twenty-five years ago, the church members in our union were reported as about 85,245; to-day they number about 276,348. Twenty-five years ago the children in our Sunday-schools were 106,711; today they are 399,317. Then the teachers were 14,600; now they are 40,216; then, as to the numbers of our London churches, there was no numerical report; now they are reported as 36,095. Then, as to chapel building, no particulars were known, and so little were we interested in this department of edification that no particulars were collected before 1864; but Mr. Alfred Bowser, who is our final authority in such matters, has favoured me with a tabulated statement, which shows that within the last *thirteen* years, in England alone, not including Ireland, Scotland, Wales, or the country of Monmouth, we have expended £1,026,099 on the erection of chapels, thus providing an increase of about 170,000 sittings.

Gentlemen, I can understand a little about material values but not much; I know the cost of buildings when I am told; I can hear Mr. Booth say that we now have sittings for 1,028,833 persons, and should be glad to find that this estimate is too small by half; but *spiritual* statistics I do not understand. I reverence the seers who write our annual books of Numbers, but for myself I never knew how to tabulate the consequences even of one single successful throw of a gospel net cast by any man, so as, like the old Galilean, to set down in my book the number of fishes caught, for instance "there—exactly one hundred and fifty and three—*three*, not quite four." I am no actuary, quick at working sums in gospel arithmetic; indeed, I think that such sums generally defy the multiplication table, and confound analysis; no calculating machine, no ready reckoner can help us much in counting conversions; and it seems to me that if the mystic man seen in the prophet's vision, "clothed in linen, and with a writer's inkhorn at his side" were to appear to us, offering to mark and tell up God's people for us, even then we should not understand what he would have to say about spiritual numbers and their value. So, if I felt sure as to the numerical accuracy of our figures to-night, I should not be sure of their true meaning. What do you mean by 276,348 sinners who repent? What do you mean by *one*? As Latimer said, "I hear a pen scratching behind the arras." It is the Lord who is even now writing up his people, but we shall not know the true census until the day when, having finished it, he shall read it out. With all these reserves, however, and all these qualifications, I do think that the rough numerical statement now given is an index of great value, furnishing proof of progress that we should joyfully recognize, and for which we should give God all the glory.

I also venture to say that we have encouragement in *the spiritual life* of our churches compared with what it was twenty-five years ago. Although we have nothing to be proud of, and much to be sorry for, the Holy Spirit, whom we have so often grieved, is working within us "to will and to do of his good pleasure." By that grace we have more mutual knowledge, more cohesive force, more active kindness in the churches of our union. I think also that Baptists better understand the essential catholicity of their distinctive principle—the principle that always puts faith *first,* and that makes union with Christ everything, so that we are only consistent with ourselves when we are "broad as the charity of Almighty God, yet narrow as his righteousness."

Going from branch to root, I hasten to mark a third encouragement to thank God for you and congratulate ourselves upon, and that is, *a growing love to the old gospel.* Let us be clear about what we mean by the old gospel, for this I am glad to hope is the live and burning question of the day. Some say the gospel is *infinite;* we say the gospel is only a *direction* to what is infinite. A direction that in itself is infinite is practically no direction at all. When it is late, and I want to know the way to this place, I am not satisfied with an infinite direction. When I am ill, and want to know how to get well, I am not satisfied with an infinite direction, so, if I am lost, and want to know this very minute, while I am slipping off the cliff of life, what I must do to be saved, I am not satisfied with an infinite direction. The gospel, however, is essentially directive, telling us all, first, what we need to know that we may *be* saved, next what we need to know when we *are* saved; speaking, not in melodious generalities, but in round and royal notes, or "writing the vision on tables, that he who runs may read," we have been told that "the gospel is an infinite truth." I allow that this saying swells with a grand sound, and that the idea conveyed, when you come to think, has that "Obscurity" in it, which Dr. Blair remarks, "is not unfavourable to the sublime." Still, for myself, I speak of the gospel as *definite,* a definite direction to infinite truth, infinite purity, infinite charity, infinite heaven, infinite illumination, and all these infinities being gradually and eternally found in the Infinite Jesus!

The theory as to the gospel being infinite rather than definite naturally leads to a fashion of language that is not definite, language which the late Archbishop [Richard] Whately compared to light in a London fog; light that is sometimes resplendent with gay prismatic colours, but which fails to show things definitely; light that is just sufficient to tempt men to keep at their business, though not enough to save them from running against a lamp post, or stumbling down a cellar. There may be a few, even of our own people, who think that love of this kind of light implies intellectual supereminence, and who dream that to be indefinite is to be broad. "You ought to be broad," say they, "Yes, indeed," say we! But we are now speaking of the gospel *road,* and that is not what the New Testament calls the "broad road." The question is, not whether we have a broad or a narrow road, but whether we have one that answers the purpose. "I would rather have a bridge narrow as Hungerford that goes right across the river than one broad as Westminster that stops in the middle."

We love "the broad land of wealth unknown," but we have no love of indefiniteness in the language of direction to it; we want more than the misty message "that Christ did something or other, which somehow or other, had some connexion or other with salvation;" for though we are many-sided, and have many sympathies, we are no "children of the mist," and have no sympathy with fog, "Ah," said Neander, "there is a future for you Baptists!" I should be sorry to think so in any influential sense apart from our fidelity to God's definite revelation of a Saviour. Indeed, I could not think so; for then the glory of the Lord would depart from our camp; but we believe that, as a rule, our pastors have a growing wish to teach and our people to learn the truth, the whole truth, and nothing but the truth of the gospel as a recorded revelation, the gospel fixed in its first meaning, and unchanged as the laws of the lens or the triangle.

II. From reporting some of the encouragements, let me go on to speak about some of the *instruments* by which they have been brought about.

Meeting in this place, and in present circumstances, you know what instrument I shall naturally mention first. Twenty-five years ago there came up to London a young Levite, whose advent was a revolution. I name no names. The youth I mean was not quite according to pattern, and while he was "determined to know nothing among men save Jesus Christ and him crucified," he said and did bold things with such racy tokens of strong individuality, and with a smile of such cheerful, cool, refreshing frankness, to say the least of it, that some of the excellent of the earth looked at him over their spectacles with wise and wary glance, felt a catch in their breath, and were nervous, not so much at what he *had* said as at what he was *going* to say. Some thought he would flare up and go out; and further on, when growing crowds assembled, and growing nobilities or work were done, some were ready to say: "Give God the praise, we know that this man is a sinner. There was but one opinion as to the fact of power: there was many as to the secret of it. As, when the question was asked to Samson: "Tell me I pray thee wherein thy great strength lieth," some persons rather thought that the strength lay in the hair, so some scientists suggested totally inadequate explanations of the strength now in question. Doubtless there were secondary causes not far to seek.

It is a great thing to have a great heart. It is a great thing, and a rare, for a man to be a man. Few persons walk on stilts, but many talk on stilts, and it is a great thing to be perfectly natural. It is a great thing for preacher to have a preaching nature; so that he can say what he likes, when he likes, and can command the happy word that strikes straight out and hits the white. It is a great thing to show no white feather, and never to run away from a lie; it is a great thing to have no secret like a lie in the life; it is a great thing to have no nerves, and to have no doubts, for whatever doubts may be good for, they are not good to preach; it is a great thing to be gifted with a voice that can flow out with tranquil power and fill with ease a place like this giving in clear sound clear sense; so that the busy, weary men of London may catch all the music and all the meaning in a moment, without a puzzle. It is a great thing in writing or speaking English to have "the unerring first touch" that marks the artist. These are great things, and these natural causes must have corresponding natural effects; but the natural can never produce the supernatural: "That which is born of the flesh is flesh."

The Holy, Sovereign Spirit alone has wrought the continuous wonder that has been witnessed here, glorifying Christ by blessing the word of Christ's servant. Through that blessing alone we have seen this place gradually become a centre of gracious activities and a vast apparatus of help to souls; so, to speak in scientific fashion, this Tabernacle has been a kind of germ-cell out of which other tabernacles have had development, and from this church hundreds of other churches have had formation. Here is a preaching station with no end to its radius. On Sunday morning, when the minister stands on this spot, he not only speaks to row beyond row within the walls, but his voice travels on till it strikes Australia. When we take into account the audience in this place, along with the 25,000 copies of each morning sermon printed on an average in England only, and the number of readers each copy has, it would be a moderate thing to say that Mr. Spurgeon preaches every week to a congregation of one hundred thousand. If, within the few minutes allotted me, I were to attempt to give a fair statement of things that show the influence of Mr. Spurgeon on our denominational growth, my statement would only daze and stun you with astounding facts rather than secure a clear appreciation of their value. In offering to you the mere statistics of surfaces it would be necessary to speak volumes.

One volume would be wanted to show his manifold influence on the churches though the press; another would be wanted to race it as conveyed through the many societies and institutions of the Tabernacle; another would be wanted to show his manifold influence on the churches through the press; another would be wanted to trace it as conveyed through the many societies and institutions of the Tabernacle; another would be wanted to follow out the workings of the Pastors' College. From this College 416 brethren have entered the ministry as recognized pastors of churches or missionaries. Of these missionaries, fifteen are in Australia or New Zealand; four in China; one is in Japan; two are in India, and another is just going; two are in the West Indies; one is at St. Helena; five are in Africa; one is in Brazil; one at Naples; two are in Spain; nineteen of the young men are now ministers in the United

States; eight are in Canada; two are in Nova Scotia. Several ladies from the Tabernacle Church are engaged in Zenana [women missionaries] or kindred work in the East Indies [India].

Reserving reports about foreign work, and still confining our references to home, allow me just to notify that 102 new churches have been founded by the students, 118 new chapels have been built or bought, much has been expended on chapel enlargements or improvements, on paying off old debts, on building new schools and manses. The secretary has just said to me, "On a very moderate estimate indeed, not including the cost of this Tabernacle, and keeping much below the actual facts, I should put down the sum laid out in buildings at £300,000." As far as figures can show the most recent facts of spiritual success, they are as follows: In the returns made in 1878 by 292 pastors only, the others not sending returns, some from diffidence, some from not understanding the request, 3,544 baptisms were reported, with a net increase of 3,124 in 292 churches. The total baptisms from 1868 to 1878 were 36,123; net increase, 33,282; and at the present time the churches presided over by ministers sent out from the Pastors' College have a total membership of 39,308.

Think of the work and responsibility which all these facts imply being carried on by Mr. Spurgeon through the intense history of twenty-five years; of his being through all that period the life of such an executive as yours, diffusing his presence through the complex machinery that has its centre here. It is more than man was made for, or than flesh and blood can bear. It would be enough to make an Atlas faint. In such a case, even the joy of success is a fearful joy. Living at such high pressure, and in the midst of such eternal publication, if there are times when his soul is struck through with the spirit of jubilee, there must also be time when to his excited fancy the powers of earth and hell are striving against him in one black fraternization, times of terrible tension, times of passionate silence, times of power only to cry, "Alone, alone!" No wonder that he has your love. Under God, that love has had a great deal to do with making him the man he is, as Jonathan's love had a great deal to do with making David the man he was. It is mean mischief to warn congregations, as some sages do, against making idols of their ministers. I never yet knew a church show a true pastor too much true love. Depend upon it he needs it all. Pray for each discouraged minister that he may not fail in any agony-point; pray for a man still more when his life looks like one long success. Homely people say of such a man, they fear that so much praise will "turn his head." Even those who have had greatest power from God have, before now, been proud of it, and that pride has gone before a fall.

The Hebrew giant who was called by John Milton "that mighty Nazarite," the story of whose life serves as a parable, who, while the Spirit of God wrought mightily in him, could do anything; he on whom once, like a black flash, a lion sprang from the thicket; he who then grasped the monster's jaws with his iron hand, and with a twist and a snap rent him in twain, and flung the dead thing back into the thicket again; he who once dashed up the gates of Gaza from their sockets, swung them over his shoulder and bounded up the hill, even he fell and became an abject weakling, tempting the heathen to think that after all, his God was dead. But thanks to the sovereign grace of the Great Unspeakable our brother has been upheld till now, and after a pause of helplessness we see him stand with us on this red-letter day, once more renewed in his spirit's youth and his body's energy, to join in the solemn shout of the churches, and to say, "O thou Preserver of men, the living, the living, he shall praise thee, as we do this day."

The subject is too large for an address, and I must now wind up in a hurry, without the possibility of doing justice to my own meaning, or of making out a complete statement of my argument, so as to glorify my God as I wish to do. We ought to remember other instruments used by the Great Worker besides that one which we have reasonably dwelt upon with particular emphasis on this particular occasion. I can only indicate some of them without attempt at enlargement. We ought to remember the instrumentality of *Sunday-schools*. In saying this, I would, if possible, speak in capitals. We ought to remember *the revival of our own denominational enterprise* in London that commenced four years before the date of which we have been thinking, and which was first marked by the erection of Bloomsbury Chapel. In such an enterprise the first steps are the great steps. I do not mean to forget Sir Morton Peto, and I shall appropriate for him the saying, "A man was famous according as he lifted up axes on the thick trees." We ought to remember *the men who were our leaders just before the period we now trace began.* Look at the names of London ministers alone for the year 1854, and you see Hinton, Steane, Stovel, Aldis, Green, Baptist Noel, Brook, Katterns, John Stevens, and a "cloud of witnesses" besides. These ministers, some of whom are still spared to us, though most of them are now numbered with the old nobility of heaven, were all men of strong conviction, pronounced theology, and holy life, whose labours, be sure, were "not in vain in the Lord," and who were all great educators of evangelists.

We ought to remember *the secret prayers and hidden lives of Christians who lived long ago.* It is God's will to give us great spiritual blessings through human instruments, but it is not his will that we should always be able to identify those instruments. There may be at this very moment a grand work going on 18,000 miles away that was once set going by something in the life of your William Lepard or Father Olney; they never dreaming of such a thing. No mortal can trace the lineage or genealogy of a spiritual success. For instance, before the world is out, it may be found that whole nations of spirits have received more good than tongue can tell through John Bunyan's instrumentality, but to whose instrumentality do we owe John Bunyan? We must, I think, trace much of it to the "three or four godly women, sitting at a door in the sun," whose joyful conversation about the things of God he overheard, and of whom he says, "They were to me as if I had found a new world, as if they were a people that dwelt alone, and were not reckoned among their neighbours." [*Grace Abounding*, section 38]

Before now, you have been astonished by reports of success "crowning the labours" of a man who in faith, in self-denial, in spiritual scholarship, and in all the things that go to make ministerial fitness, is only one in the great multitude of the unremarkable. Yet he tells you of "*his* conversations," and you read in the papers from time to time that "he is doing a great work!" Is he? For my own part, I am inclined to think that he is only reaping what was sown by some weeping prophet who lived in former times, and whose name will be a secret until "the day shall declare it." Cardinal Newman said last week, "Most men, if they do any good, die without knowing it," and I think that the truth certainly tends in this direction. Many of the encouragements that we have been thanking God for may be the outcome and the flower of life that passed away a hundred years ago, the life of persons whose fame, when they were here, never spread more than a thousand square yards, of persons who are gone without ever having left their initials, of persons who are unknown as the anonymous angel of Gethsemane. Perhaps some of these encouragements may be given in answer to the prayer and in blessing on the life of some person whose last days were spent in some home like that which your love would endow to-day. The very first woman in all history named as speaking about "the redemption" was an old lady who lived in a retreat; and you may find all about it in the second chapter of Luke's gospel. It would be only like the Saviour to bless the lives of his hidden ones in making them instruments of cheering his churches, and who knows how much of the splendid public blessing for which to-day we thank him may be the result of prayer offered from the shade, and of lives sacred to humility.

We ought, after all, to remember that our best instruments are *instruments only*. Who, then, is Mr. Spurgeon, and who are these instruments, "but ministers by whom ye believed, even as the Lord gave to every man"? We must not boast, even if we are prosperous lest God arrest our prosperity in the hour of our pride. The sword must not boast, the trowel must not boast; to borrow Philip Henry's words, "All our songs must be sung to this humble tune: 'Not unto us, O Lord, not unto us, but unto thy name be all the glory.'"

Robert Hall has said, "It is one thing to stop, another to finish." Now, I must stop, *you* must finish; you and your children and your children's children, you, yet not you but Christ living in you. You members of a small battalion in God's great army, join with all the soldiers of the cross of every name, and begin a new "fight of faith" to-day! We have had encouragements, but is there nothing to be said on the other side? We speak of increase, but does it correspond with the increase of the general population, and is the church gaining ground on the world? We rejoice to have many new places of worship, and to know that many of them are filled, but how many "houses of Baal are filled from end to end?" We report more ministers, but how many ministers and missionaries of sin are in the field?

Three hundred years ago a preacher said to his congregation, "Shall I tell you who the diligentest bishop in all England [is]? It is the devil." Has that bishop less to do now? Is it true that the wealth of the country, contrasted with twenty-five years ago, has increased fourfold, while, speaking generally, our missionary offerings during the same period have increased onefold only? Is it true that in the course of the last twenty-five years the amount annually expended on intoxication drinks has increased from thirty to over one hundred and forty-seven millions sterling? If these things are true, then what has been done is only a beginning. Let the joy of the Lord be your strength for fresh endeavours.

Cleave to the Lord with purpose of heart"; live the life that is eternal; not in lip-language mainly, but in all the languages you know preach the great salvation. If you are Christians, never keep your Christianity a secret, but out with it; never go back, never say die! "Do good," as says Jeremy Taylor, "then do it again." In the name of the Lord, in the power of the Spirit, in the highest sense of the word, "heal the sick, cast out devils; freely ye have received, freely give."

COMMENTS

Mr. SPURGEON said: Whilst Dr. Stanford was reading that marvelous paper I felt as if it were almost a wicked thing for me to be allowed to do it; he seemed to be straining himself at such a rate to be heard, and his whole soul was thrown into it so fervently, that I now fear that he may afterwards suffer in consequence. I am sure I may say concerning our beloved brother that we only wish he had lungs and voice that could make ten thousand people hear him, for his message is worthy of the largest possible audiences. His rich thought often sets those going who make the thousands hear, besides finding spiritual meat for many of the Lord's people scattered all over the world. May his body prosper and be in health even as his soul prospers. Before you go to the business of the evening we will sing our Tabernacle National Anthem, which a critic has called that execrable tune "Cranbrook" to that glorious hymn: "Grace, 'it's a charming sound."

I am such a heretic as to like Cranbrook; and if you will only sing it as we generally sing it we will make some of these heathen here to-night like it. The way of singing now (continued Mr. Spurgeon, in affected tones to imitate the parties to whom he alluded) is "Let us sing to the praise and glory of God, and rattle through it as fast as possible, with never a fugue or a repeat, and get it over and done, for we are sick to death of it." In truth, I think some of the much admired modern tunes might be very well represented under the following story: "I hope you enjoyed our music this morning," said a gentleman of the High Church to a Presbyterian friend who was staying with him. "Well, I cannot say that I enjoy your form of service at all, I like things much better as we have them in the old kirk." "No? But now you are after all a gentleman of musical taste, did you not very much enjoy that *introit*." "I really don't know which it was." "But you must have been pleased with that *anthem,"* repeated the High Churchman. "I don't know, I can't say much in its favor," was the reply. "Well, there was one tune very remarkable, didn't you notice it? The music is very remarkable indeed." "Oh," was the response, "I didn't think much of it." "Well, now I am very sorry, because that is a very ancient tune; a tune that was sung in the early Church very often; indeed I believe it was sung in the Catacombs."

"I have even heard that this remarkable piece of music came from the Jews, and was no doubt chanted in the Liturgical service of the Temple; for you know the worship of the ancient Temple was Liturgical and not your bare Presbyterian form at all. There appears to be scarcely any doubt that the remarkable tune of this morning was originally sung by David himself when he played on his harp." "Dear me," said the Presbyterian, "I never heard that before, and it throws great light upon Scripture. I never before could make out why Saul threw a javelin at David, but if that was the tune which he sang to his harp I can understand Saul's ferocity, and justify it too." "Cranbrook" is not the tune that was sung by David, but it is a good deal better than David ever sang; the tune is more musical, and the hymn more gospel in it than was known under the law.

"Grace, 'tis a charming sound," was then sung to "Cranbrook," as only a Tabernacle audience of 6,000 people can sing it.

10. Presentation of the Testimonial by Mr. William Olney, 1879 (*MV*)

THE call of our beloved pastor from this pulpit last Lord's Day morning and evening was an exceedingly welcome and grateful one. The tenour of these sermons which I hope everyone in this place will read when they are published was an ascription on his part and from his point of view, of hearty thanksgiving and praise to God for the help rendered to him for the past twenty-five years. Standing here tonight as your representative, I wish on the behalf of the church and congregation worshipping within these walls, to make an equally emphatic and distinct acknowledgment of the goodness of our God to us. We do not disparage for a moment the valuable services which we have received from our beloved pastor, but we must remember, and I trust we do remember every one of us tonight, that our thanks are first of all to be given to the Giver of all good, who gave us our pastor, who made him what he is, and who has continued to supply him with grace and strength needful for his day from the period of the commencement of his ministry until now.

I believe there stands in this tabernacle tonight an unseen presence. We know he is here, and we would have every one of our hearts opened to his piercing inspection, so that he may clearly read therein a grateful acknowledgment to him, our Heavenly Father, for the great boon conferred on us in the gift of our beloved minister, in the grace that he has bestowed on him, and in the abundant blessing which he has given to his ministry here during the last twenty-five years. We ought to say as a church and people most emphatically in reference to the work of our pastor: "What hath God wrought?" not "What hath our pastor wrought?" I shall have the privilege of speaking to Mr. Spurgeon presently, and I shall have the privilege of speaking to him, I believe, in accordance with the will of God in a different strain from that in which I am speaking now, but I wish most distinctly on the part of you all to give the most clear and emphatic statement of our hearty thanksgiving and gratitude *to God*, a thanks which words are unable to express, for his abounding goodness and mercy toward us as a church and people.

To enumerate the many mercies received through the ministry of our pastor would be totally impossible; words are inadequate to express them. I will only allude to one. There is in this tabernacle tonight a large body of people who we owe their first knowledge of Jesus to our beloved minister: God only knows how many. Last night Mr. Spurgeon told us that during the twenty-five years of his ministry there have been added to the church fellowship upwards of nine thousand persons. Out of that nine thousand persons a very large proportion was men and women brought to a saving knowledge of the truth through Mr. Spurgeon's instrumentality. In the remembrance of this glorious text, a text emphatically insisted upon from this pulpit, "Not by might, nor by power, but by my Spirit saith the Lord of hosts," I ask you *by whom* this work has been done? I do not ask you by what instrument. *It has been done by our God,* and to our God let the honour and praise be given. Whilst we honour the man tonight, we honour him in a different spirit to that in which one was spoken of in olden time. Our cry tonight is not "It is not the voice of a man, but the voice of a God." No, we repudiate any such idea as that. Our cry is not "to our pastor be the glory and the honour;" but the glory and the honour be ascribed to Him who gave him to us, who has sustained him, and who will, we trust, keep him faithful for many a year, until the "golden wedding" comes. May you be here to see it?

After the very able paper of Mr. Carr, it will not be necessary for me to say much about our pastor. But one point demands most explicit utterance tonight, a point upon which he has been greatly misunderstood. The generosity of our pastor; his self-abnegation, and his self-denial, I will speak of from a deacon's point of view. I should like it to be clearly understood for I know the words I utter will be heard beyond this place and beyond the audience now listening. I should like it to be understood that after twenty-five years intimate fellowship with him on money matters, I can testify to this one thing: whilst the world says concerning him that he has made a good thing of it by becoming the minister of this Tabernacle, I can say it is *we* that have made a good thing of it, and *not he*. The interests of this church have always been first with him, and personal interests have always been second. Now, facts are stubborn things. Let me give you a few of them. When he first came at the invitation of the church, we were a few feeble folk; the sittings at Park Street had for some years gone a begging; the minister' salary was exceedingly small, and the difficulty we had in keeping the doors open was very great. Incidental and other expenses of one sort and another were a heavy burden upon the people.

When Mr. Spurgeon came the arrangement between him and the deacons was that whatever the seat rents produced should be his. Those seat rents had been supplemented in the case of all former pastorates by a great number of collections, and the hat had to go round frequently, a few having to give at the end of the year to keep matters straight. When Mr. Spurgeon came, the seats went begging no longer. The seat rents as they come in, all belonged to him. Did he keep them? No! The first thing he did at the close of three month was to say, "Now we will have no more collections for incidental expenses. I will pay for the cleaning and lighting myself;" and from that time until now he has done so. There has never been a collection for the current incidental expenses in this Tabernacle, and I believe there never will be as long as he lives, I hope not until the end of time.

Now for another important fact. There was what we might fairly call an interregnum between the time that this church was worshipping in New Park Street, and its removal here. During those three years we were wandering in some senses of the word. At one part of the time we worshipped in Exeter Hall, and also in the Surrey Music Hall. During the whole of that time the crowds collected to hear our pastor in such numbers that certain charges were made for admission to the several buildings. Tickets called preference tickets were issued in large numbers for the privileges of early admission to hear Mr. Spurgeon, and the whole of the proceeds legitimately belonged to him. Did he take them? Not one farthing. I speak from the book, mind, and such facts ought to be made known on such nights as these. During those three years Mr. Spurgeon paid over to the treasury of this church for the building of this Tabernacle just upon £5,000, all of which belonged to him, for he was fairly and clearly entitled to it. That is what we have received at the hand of our pastor. Now listen again. Our pastor says, "That will do," but it will not do for me, and I do not believe that it will do for you. I want this to be heard outside this Tabernacle. The news of this great meeting will be in the newspapers, and be read by many who do not understand Mr. Spurgeon and who do not understand us; and I wish the entire world, reporters and everybody else, clearly to understand that I am speaking facts which can be demonstrated and proved.

The most generous helper of all the institutions connected with this place of worship for many years has been Mr. Spurgeon. He has set us an example of giving. He has not stood to preach to us here for what he has got by preaching, but he has set an example to every one of us, to show that every institution here must be maintained in full vigour and strength. The repairs in connection with this place of worship, the maintenance of it, the management of all its institutions and of everything connected with the building and the property, and everything else has been under his fostering care. Not only so, but the proceeds to which he was fully entitled have never been taken by him from the first day until now, and he does not take them at the present moment. But instead of that, I will tell you what he does. He told you at our public meeting, and if he had not told it then it deserves to be told a dozen times over. He has expended upon the Lord's work so much of what he has received for preaching in the Tabernacle, that he has during some of the years returned as much as he received. This does not represent all we owe to him, and it is putting our obligation to him on a very low scale indeed. What we owe to him as a church

God only knows. Why, sir, there are hearts here that love you with an intense affection; an affection which eternity only will reveal to you. We shall have to tell you when time is no more, of the benefit and blessings conferred on our souls within these walls, and conferred on us as a church and congregation, for words want to express such obligations as these.

I have now to perform an exceedingly pleasant duty, and I will do it without troubling you any more, though this is a theme on which one might go on for a long time yet. But I will turn at once away from this matter which you will read a great deal more about, I dare say, in the paper that is to be published; and I will, as your representative, speak to our pastor, and beg in your name that he will accept the testimonial which it has been our privilege and pleasure to raise for him and to put at his absolute disposal, to commemorate the very happy event which has gathered us together in this tabernacle tonight. In the matter of this testimonial, let it go forth to the world, (I know that I am anticipating what he is going to say himself, but I cannot help it; he gave it to us last night, and it is too good to let him speak of it alone; in the matter of this testimonial,) he says "Not one farthing for me. You may give it me for myself if you like, but I will not keep it. It shall all be the Lord's, and all belong to the Lord's cause." Many of you know how it is going to be appropriated, or he will tell you presently as to that point; but still it has been raised by you as an expression of your love for him, and I have to hand it over to him in the name of the deacons and in the name of the committee, to be at his absolute disposal, as a gift without conditions, and as an expression of our great attachment to him and love for him.

Now, my dear pastor, will you please accept that gift from us, not so much for what it is as for what it represents. We should like that you should hear in that gift certain voices. Let me speak for these voices. First of all, we want you to hear the voice of your deacons. They had the pleasure and privilege of originating the subscription to the testimonial fund, and the large sums which they were enabled to place at the head of the testimonial money list, and the large help which they were enabled to render it at the outset gave such an impetus and stimulus to the movement, that it went ahead and rolled along pleasantly and easily until it was done. I am sure that the pleasure you will have in receiving this testimonial at the hands of my beloved brethren and colleagues, the deacons with the rest of the friends, does not at all equal the joy and satisfaction which we have in raising it for you, and in now asking you to accept it from us. Whilst the deacons have been unanimous in their determination to do honour to our beloved pastor in this matter, there is one of them who stands preeminent, and whose name must be mentioned to-night, for indefatigable zeal and for indomitable perseverance, to whose the success of this testimonial is greatly indebted. I allude to our beloved and honoured brother, Mr. [W. C.] Murrell. His voice, sir, combines with the voices of all of his brethren to say in that testimonial, "Dear pastor, we love you."

Likewise, sir, I trust that you will also hear the voice of your elders: brethren beloved in the Lord, equally zealous to show you honour, and equally desirous to show to all the friends to the best of their ability, how much they desire to magnify the grace of God in you, and to cooperate with you in the good work of the Lord here. Likewise, I am thankful to say that this testimonial is the contribution of all the members of the church. I believe there is not one of you, dear friends, but has been represented in some way or other in this testimonial. I am glad it is so. And I am also glad to say, that, whilst we have received one sum of £250, which is the largest donation that we have had, we have received the pence, and in some cases the farthings that were freely given. Not only, sir, does it represent the voice of the members of the church, but represents what is to you, I am sure, an exceeding joyous and happy portion of your people, and that is, the workers amongst us. If you could have seen the bazaar, you would have found almost every one of them distinguished by some peculiar title, not representing a single person, but representing such agencies as these "Sunday School," "Bible Classes," male and female, (these had six or eight stalls); "College Evangelist," "Mr. Bartlett's Class," "Butchers' Festival Committee," "Mrs. Allison and her Class," "Missionary Working Society," "Evangelists' Association," "Training Class," "Country Mission," "Evangelistic Choir," "Flower Mission," "Richmond Street Mission," and "Mansfield Street Sunday School." All these are in great sympathy with this work and did their utmost to show their great love for you. In fact there was but one feeling amongst us, we each tried to outvie the other; none wanted to be second in this matter, no, not even the youngest; and we were all ever glad indeed to have a share in this pleasure. Among the voices that speak to you today are those of the ministers and students of the Pastor's College and of the master and matrons and boys of the Stockwell Orphanage.

These are exceedingly pleasant voices to you when they say, as they emphatically do, by earnest and vigorous effort and by generous gift, "Dear Sir, we love you: we love you." These do not represent all the givers to that testimonial, for there were many others besides.

The list of stall-keepers I have not completed but you have the list of love in *The Sword and the Trowel*, and therein you will find "of honourable women not a few." Among these were several of your friends, not connected with our church and congregation, but who, as readers of your sermons, and from their deep affection for you, felt they also must help us in doing you honour. Among these were our friends of the Butchers' Festival Committee, represented by Mrs. Matthews and Mrs. Clayton; and by Mrs. Mansell, and Mrs. Withers, of Reading. I cannot forget at this present moment, and it would be wrong of me to do so, that over one of the stalls in the bazaar there were these words, "Mrs. Spurgeon's stall." On that stall there was but one class of articles, articles prepared by the loving wife of the pastor; and there at that stall stood two young men, serving the product of a mother's loving, skillful hands. From that stall, sir, there came things of beauty which to many of us will be "a joy forever," and which are adorning our walls as mementoes of affection for her who made them. Within those beautiful silken frames many of us have now a portrait on which when we look our hearts burn with joy and thankfulness, and will do so as long as we shall live.

But, sir, I cannot but remember that may a loved one has gone who otherwise would have been here to-night. During the last five and twenty years many a devoted adherent of this church exceedingly fond of you has passed away from time into eternity. If there is sympathy and communion between the world beyond the river and this lower state, I can fancy those sainted spirits are hovering here, joining in our holy festivities, and I trust that in this testimonial, although personally they have had no hand in it, you will hear their loving voices saying, "Pastor, we loved you once: we love you still."

But, better still, I trust that in that testimonial there will be a still small voice coming into your inmost soul, spoken by no human lips, but by Him whose you are and whom you serve: I trust that you will hear those loving words, "I have loved thee with an everlasting love." "Lo, I am with you even unto the end of the world;" and I hope that the grace which has sustained you so long, and made you so useful, will still rest upon you, and the power of the Holy Spirit be vouchsafed to you, that many a day of usefulness may yet be in store for you. May your brother's wish expressed just now be more than realised. May you be here at the golden wedding, even if some of us are elsewhere, and may the testimonial then presented to you be more complete and larger, but as loving as the one we present to you to-night, which we ask your acceptance of with great joy and gladness.

The amount of the testimonial is £6,233, and the whole sum is now at our pastor's absolute disposal, as the testimonial which you have presented to him.

COMMENTS

Mr. JAMES A. SPURGEON: My dear brother, William Olney, has not presented the clock yet. Now, it does so happen that whilst he is the senior deacon of the church, I am the co-pastor of it. Therefore, I just take my honourable position for the moment, and step in and supply that little lack of service. I can perfectly endorse all that has been said concerning this church by our brother William Olney. Every voice that he has referred to, and ten thousand other voices, speak in this testimonial; and I hope that my brother will be able to listen to those voices, if there should ever come any seasons of retirement again, which God spare him from. (Voices: "Amen, amen.") When there shall be a silence that is felt, I hope that these gentle musical voices will ring out in his ear, and teach his heart the exceeding great love of this people towards him, as their pastor. This testimonial is given to him. He takes nothing, I know, for him; but we do ask him to take to himself this clock and the ornaments. May they be in his study until his golden wedding, and may they come here again at that jubilee, and we will look at them. I hope that the clock will enable him to maintain his constant habit of always being in time and may be always, if I may be allowed a pun, a *striking token of your regard for him.*

Mr. SPURGEON was received in manner which no one who was present will ever forget, and which those who were not present cannot imagine. After some considerable time had passed he spoke as follows:

I should hope, dear friends, that I am not expected to make any reply, because it really would be to expect what must be impossible. I thank you very, very, very heartily for this testimonial, and I hope that you will not consider that I do not take it to myself and use it personally because I hand it over to works over charity, for my Lord's work is dear to me, and to use it for him and for his poor is the sweetest way of using it for myself. I said at the very first that, if a testimonial could be made the means of providing for our aged sisters in the Almshouse I would be doubly glad to receive it; and when friends urged that they had rather give *to me*, I begged them to let me have my own way, *for surely a man may have his way on his silver-wedding day* if at no other time. The matter was commenced on that footing, but I never dreamed that you would give anything like this right royal amount. Our communion fund has been so heavily drawn upon by the support of the almswomen that we have been embarrassed in providing for the very large number of poor persons, who, I am thankful to say, belong to this church. I hope we shall always have a large number of the Lord's poor among us, for thus we are able to show kindness unto our Lord himself. We erected more almsrooms than we had money for, and I felt it to be wrong to leave the church in future years with these endowed houses, for time might come when this extra burden could not be borne, since in these days of our strength we find it a load. For such an object I heartily approved of an endowment. Endowments for the support of ministers are confessedly a great evil, since they enable a man to keep among a people long after his usefulness is over; but no such evil can arise in the present instance. £5,000 was considered by our dear friend Mr. Greenwood, who is my invaluable guide in such matters, to be about sufficient for our object. Therefore £5,000 of this noble testimonial is hereby devoted to that end.

You must know that, from the first, my brethren the deacons were of the mind that I ought to accept whatever you gave me for myself; but I was not of that mind. We have occasionally differed about such things, and it has generally been in the same direction, for they never stint me; the bounds are set by myself. Well, when it came to pass that there was £6,200, and then our brethren kindly said, "Now you ought to take that £1,200. The friends meant it for you, and they will not like it unless you do." Well, now dear friends, you must please like it, because I really will not take anything of it. It is a testimonial of gratitude to God for twenty-five years of happy communion and prosperity, and unto God let the testimonial go, all of it, with the one exception of a bronze clock for my study, which I will accept as a memorial of the fond affection of my dear people towards me. The price of that memorial will come out of the amount, and I propose to let the rest lie with Mr. Greenwood and Mr. Thomas Olney for the very short time which will elapse between tonight and the drawing of it out. The treasurers will have the money, and they will certify you that it goes as I have described. There will be no need for persons to besiege me with begging letters, as I see scores of ways for disposing of this money and much more. I mean to give a goodly portion to Mrs. Spurgeon's fund, which supplies our poorer ministers with libraries, and so finds them with help in their studies. No better work than this was ever undertaken.

The Colportage needs help, the Poor Fund of the church is £100 behindhand, and the expense of the late Special Services have not been fully met, and so all will be needed.

But there is one thing to which £50 must be devoted. I mentioned last night that the honoured founder of our Boys' Orphanage has sent £50 for a Girls' Orphanage: to this we must add our £50, and announce that the subscription list has now commenced.

Do not be afraid, for I have no present intent of drawing upon you for this work; it will lie quiet for a while, and silently grow if the Lord so pleases. These opportunities of consecrating our substance are great blessings in themselves, and secure a blessing upon the rest of our possessions. God's providence can soon take away from the niggardly man a hundred times more than he can save by his miserliness. Speak of bleeding you for money, a few leeches in the form of bank shares, or Turkish bonds, would soon have sucked a hundred times more than works of piety and charity even suggest to you.

I propose further that as certain bales of goods remain over from the bazaar, these shall be sold on June 19th next, my birthday, at the Stockwell Orphanage, and the proceeds shall go to the Girls' Orphanage fund, which is hereby commenced. So far as the disposal of the money is concerned this matter is ended, but it never will be ended as far as my grateful recollections of you are concerned.

Mr. William Olney said more than enough about what I have done in money matters. I will only add that I serve a good Master, and am so sure that he will provide for me that I never thought it worth my while to be scraping and hoarding for myself. When I gave myself up at first to be his minister, I never expected anything beyond food and raiment, and when my income was £45 a year I was heartily content, and never thought of a need without having it supplied. It is with me much the same now: "I have all things and abound." I have only one grievance, and that is, being asked for loans and gifts of money when

I have none to spare. Under the impression that I am a very rich man many hunt me perpetually, but I wish these borrowers and beggars to know that I am not rich. They argue that a man must be rich if he gives away large sums, but in my case this is just the reason why I am not rich. When I have a spare £5, the College, or Orphanage, or Colportage, or something else, requires it, and away it goes. I could very comfortably do with much more. O that I could do more for Christ, and more for the poor. For these I have turned beggar before now and shall not be ashamed to beg again. The outside world cannot understand that a man should be moved by any motive except that of personal gain; but, if they knew the power of love to Jesus, they would understand that greed of wealth is vile as the dust beneath his feet to the lover of the Saviour.

I do not think your affectionate congratulations and hearty cheers will elate me, for I am better aware of my faults and failings than you are, and, moreover, if anybody has praised me in public, my Master, if he sees me lifted up, will give me such a whipping behind the door that I shall be more like to cry than to crow. Conceit is very apt to grow, but our Lord keeps it under with a sharp rod; and yet we ought not to need such sharp discipline, for pride in such weak creatures is folly, in such weak creatures is falsehood. I say no more.

I beg you to pray very much for me that I may be held up for years to come. I shall be, by the Lord's grace. We stand on a rock which does not move. We have a gospel to preach which is not exhausted, and we trust in a Spirit who never deserts those that confide in him. We are not afraid for the future, but, brethren, pray for us more than ever, for your prayers are our riches.

And, would to God that there were some here tonight who have been expressing by their applause their affection to their minister, who would ask themselves whether they have any love to Jesus Christ or not. What you have given me tonight is valuable, but I would rather have you than yours. I would rather that you were brought to Christ than that you brought your money to his servant. I pray that you may give yourselves up to the dear Redeemer and put your trust in him and you shall find him to be as good to you as he has been to me.

Beloved friend, this last word, the tie which unites us is quite unlike that which usually exists between minister and people: we are truly and heartily one. My deacons and elders who work with me are my brothers in very truth. We have no stately modes of address, but I am profanely called "the governor"; and there are "brother Williams" and other playful names among us. These brethren are some of them esquires, who ought also to be [Members of Parliament]; but we love them too well to dignify them. We are all brethren, most heartily so. I said to an elder of the church this evening. "You can run about, but I must totter, for I have not got your legs." He replied, "I would cheerfully let you have them dear sir, and take your weak ones, if I could help you in any way." I know he meant it, too. One day I said a sharp word or two to a brother, and I think he deserved it; but he said to me, "Well, that may be so, but I will tell you what, sir. I would die for you any day." "Oh," I said, "bless your heart, I am sorry I was so sharp, but still you did deserve it, did you not?" He smiled and said he thought he did, and there the matter ended.

Well, this love is to me an amazement. I am the most astonished person among you. I do not comprehend it. It seems a romance to me. *What I have done I shall do still, namely: love you with all my heart, and love my Lord as his grace enables me. I mean to go on preaching Jesus, and his gospel and you may be sure that I shall not preach anything else, for it is with me Christ or nothing. I am sold up, and my stock in trade is gone if Jesus Christ is gone. He is the sum of my ministry, my all in all.*

Now, you will please to understand that I mean all that you would mean if *you* were in my position; and I beg again to thank you most heartily, every one of you, especially the dear friends who read us the papers, especially those who listened to them, and especially everybody.

(The hymn "Art thou weary?" having been sung Mr. Spurgeon mentioned valuable gifts of friends who wish to be unknown; and he also intimated that a friend, who did not approve of endowments, had sent £25 for the Colportage; while another, finding himself too late, had promised suits for six orphans and £25 for the Girls' Orphanage. Mr. Spurgeon thought it time to go home, for fear he should be overwhelmed with more of such offerings; and so the benediction was pronounced, the doxology was sung and the feast of brotherly love was over).

SOLI DEO GLORIA.

Appendix A:
"Our Motto is, 'Go forward and never step back.'"

"We must go from strength to strength, and be a missionary church, and never rest until not only this neighbourhood, but our country, of which it is said that some parts are as dark as India, shall be enlightened with the gospel." (CHS)

1. "The Ceremony of Laying the First Stone of the New Tabernacle." Tuesday, August 16, 1859 (*MB*)

Pastor C. H. Spurgeon offered the Opening Prayer after the singing of the 100th Psalm:

"O LORD God! Thy throne is in heaven. Yet heaven and the heaven of heavens cannot contain thee, neither can any among the sons of men build a house for thy habitation and thy rest. The temple of Solomon, however beautiful for the situation, glorious for its splendour and "exceeding magnifical," was not fit for thy dwelling place. It is not possible that thou who fillest immensity, thou who dwellest in light to which no man can approach, should confine thyself to temples piled with human hands. Nevertheless thou hast said, "To this man also will I look, even to him that is poor and of a contrite spirit, and trembleth at my Word." Jesus, Master of Assemblies, where two or three are gathered together in thy name, there art thou in the midst of them. Blessed Comforter, without thy quickening influence, the largest congregation is but a listless crowd, the most gorgeous cathedral but a profane place. Thou has been pleased, O Lord, to increase thy people and to multiply their joy. We have had the joy of harvest, and the shoutings as of them that tread the wine-press. Thou hast been greatly with us, and thy right arm has been made bare in the eyes of all the people. And now behold, this day we are come together to lay the first stone of a house for thee, wherein we may meet for thy sacred worship. Oh, give us the first drops of a shower of mercy! Oh that this day every one concerned in the laying of this stone may partake of the blessing of the Most High. Bless the church that shall assemble in it! May we find our richest expectations far exceed, and our firmest hope far excelled. Do thou, O God, bless the many thousands that we hope will gather here, and grant that the Word may be quick and powerful to their conversion. We know that places cannot be consecrated; yet can there be consecrated associations connected with them. Lord give us the fullness of thy blessing at the beginning; and as we progress, and stone mounts on stone, may we come at last to know the better is the end of a thing than the beginning thereof. God bless thy servant who is about to lay this first stone! We thank thee for him, and we pray thee bless him abundantly. Grant that the wealth and station thou has conferred upon him may be ever, as they have been, fully consecrated unto thee. And do thou bless all the dear brethren of the ministry now present. Oh, grant to every one of them the fullness of thy Spirit, and the joy of thy salvation, and the light of thy countenance. And bless we beseech thee, the assembled congregation. This very day may sinners be converted and glorified and God be glorified. And now, thou who dost bow thine ear to listen to our requests, hearken to our prayer, while we beseech thee to let this house be builded without accident, let no hindrance when builded may it by the manifestation of thy presence to the saints be filled with thy glory. And for many years to come, yea until the Second Advent, thou long-expected Messiah, may ministers of a full, free, and finished salvation, occupy its pulpit. And unto Father, Son, and Holy Ghost be glory forever. Amen."

(The stone was laid by Sir Morton Peto, M.P., and the following articles were placed under the foundation stone: The Bible, The Old

Baptist Confession of Faith, signed by Benjamin Keech; Declaration of the Deacons, printed on parchment; an edition of Dr. [John] Rippon's Hymn Book; and Programme of the day's Proceedings.)

2. Prayer of Pastor John Spurgeon [father of C. H. Spurgeon] in the Evening Meeting of the Ceremony of Laying the First Stone of the New Tabernacle, 1859 (*MB*)

"O bless us all, and bless thy young servant [C. H. Spurgeon]. Do thou stand by him and keep him from the mighty foes against whom he has to contend. Keep far from him the influence of sin and Satan, and may he find joy and peace in God. O Our Father, keep him, O keep him; let him not be lifted up by what he has seen, or by what thou has done for him today. Oh, do thou keep his soul humble, and then he will always be strong to praise thy great and holy name. Oh, may he draw from the fountain which is full, which runneth over, and may he find that the God of peace and love is continually with him. Bless his church and congregation; O Father, smile upon them, we leave them in thy hands; we seek thy favour and presence with us tonight. Grant, great God, that sinners may be converted unto thee. There are some in thy presence who are a few steps from the grave, some hastening on the abyss of woe, walking with the giddy multitude in the way which leads to death and eternal destruction. God save them! Oh, pluck them as brands from the eternal burning. May thine all-sufficient grace turn their hearts, and thy name be glorified. Bless everyone now present. Prepare us for this service, accept our song of praise, and fill our hearts with joy, for the dear Redeemer's sake. Amen."

3. C. H. Spurgeon's Comments at the "Meeting of our own Church," at the Metropolitan Tabernacle, Newington, Monday, April 8, 1861 (*MB*)

Comments of C. H. Spurgeon:

"I do not think, that in the course of the next twenty years, you, as a Church, will have such a choice of pastors as you have had during the last twenty years. If I should die you can do so, I suppose, but I do not think that anything short of that, would get me to go away from this spot. I hardly agree with ministers when they get beaten, showing the white feather and resigning the charge. I feel I am captain of the vessel, and if there should be Jonah in the ship I shall as gently, and in as Christian a spirit as possible, pitch him out; I shall not think, because Jonah is there that therefore I ought to get out, but stand by the ship in ill weather as well as in sunshine. I know that by God's grace I was called to this place; and if God's grace and providence shall move me, well and good, but nothing else ever will. I have not the slightest doubt but that, as our numbers shall increase, in answer to earnest prayer, the Spirit of God will be poured out yet more abundantly upon the minister and the people, and that we, being bound together yet more surely in ties of affection and in ties of hearty cooperation, may go from strength to strength in glorifying God and serving one another. Why should not this ancient Church become as glorious in the future as in the past? O may God hear our prayers and it must be so. Jesus shall here be honoured and the truth maintained."

Appendix B:
Thomas Olney (1790–1869), "A Father to the Minister," and William Olney, "Senior Deacon (and Elder)"

1. Testimonial to Thomas Olney, Opening of the Metropolitan Tabernacle, 1861 (*MB*)

Thomas Olney [was] connected with the Church for fifty-one years as a member, and twenty-two years as a deacon. Mr. Olney has been of great use to the Church in many ways during the long time he has been connected with it, and had rendered it most important service as its treasurer. Mr. Olney was a father to the Minister, and a sleepless guardian of the Church. Such a deacon few Churches possessed, and a better was never chosen. He joyed in their joy, and sorrowed in their sorrow. Abuse fell to the pastor's lot sometimes, but his kind deacons and elders always had a cheering word. He was told they were singing songs about him (Mr. Spurgeon) in the street. He was sure that if any poor man could get a halfpenny by abusing him, he hoped that he would carry on his trade.

The following is a copy of the Testimonial:

"The Baptized Church of Jesus Christ, under the pastoral care of Rev. C. H. Spurgeon.

At the Annual Church Meeting, held on Wednesday, January 16, 1861, the following Resolution was proposed, seconded, and carried unanimously:

"That this Church desires to record its devout gratitude of Almighty God, for the abundant grace which has preserved our dear and honoured brother, Thomas Olney, as a consistent, useful, and beloved member of this Church for the lengthened period of 51years. And while to the grace of God all the varied excellencies of our brother are to be ascribed, the pastor, officers, and Church members cannot refrain from returning unfeigned and hearty thanks to our brother, for his indefatigable labours as a deacon for 22 years, and for his most valuable services as treasurer. No man can be more truly worthy of the esteem of his Christian brethren, and we most earnestly invoke a blessing upon him, upon our beloved sister [Unity, (d) 1863] the partner of his life, and upon his godly family, which is by so many ties united with us as a people. We trust that in that great House of Prayer, over every stone of which he has watched so anxiously, he may be spared to see the largest wishes of his heart fulfilled in the gathering of immense assemblies, the salvation of many souls, and the daily increase of our numbers as a Church."

Signed on behalf of the Church, by the Pastor, Deacons and Elders.

2. "The Good Deacon" by C. H. Spurgeon, June 1868 *(S&T)*

Of late years we have heard a great deal against deacons and have read discussions as to their office, evidently suggested by no idolatrous reverence for their persons. Many of our ministering brethren bitterly rate them, others tremble at the mention of their very name, and few put on their armour and prepare to do battle with them wherever they go, as if they were dragons of ministerial life. *We* ourselves are charged with having said that "a deacon is worse than a devil, for if you resist the devil he will flee from you, but if you resist a deacon he will fly at you." This is no saying of ours, we never had any cause to speak so severely, and although in some cases it is undoubtedly true, we have never had any experimental proof of it. Not one in a hundred of all the sayings fathered upon us are ours at all, and as to this one it was vogue before we were born. Our observation of deacons leads us to observe that, as rule, they are quite as good men as the pastors, and the bad and good in the ministry and the deaconate are to be found in very much the same proportions. If there be lordly deacons, are there not lordly pastors? If there be ignorant, crotchety men among deacons, are there not their rivals in our pulpits?

The church owes an immeasurable debt of gratitude to those thousands of godly men who study her interests day and night, contribute largely of their substance, care for her poor, cheer her ministers, and in times of trouble as well as prosperity remain faithfully at their posts. Whatever there may be here and there of mistake, infirmity, and even wrong, we assured from wide and close observation, that the greater numbers of our deacons are an honour to our faith, and we may style them as the apostle did his brethren, the "glory of Christ." Heaviest censure is occasionally deserved, but affectionate esteem is usually due. Deprive the church of her deacons and she would be bereaved of her most valiant sons; their loss would be the shaking of the pillars of our spiritual house, and would cause desolation on every side. Thanks be to God such a calamity did not likely to befall us, for the great Head of the church in mercy to her, will always raise up a succession of faithful men, who will use the office well, and earn unto themselves a good degree and much boldness in the faith. Much ought to be taken into consideration in estimating the character of men sustaining office in the church, for many difficulties may be incidental to the position, and this may mitigate the severity with which we ought to judge the men. Our brethren in the deacon's work are not as migratory as our ministers; they are frequently born to Christ in the churches in which they live and die; they cannot readily remove when evil days becloud the church, but remain chained to the oar to bear the odium of discontent and the sorrow of decay. No frequent removal secures for them renewal of popularity elsewhere; their whole career for bad or good is remembered by one and the same constituency, and hence false steps are with great difficulty retrieved, and awkward disagreements are painfully remembered.

With new ministers come new ways, and men in office, especially elderly men, cannot so easily learn and unlearn as young and fresh comers might desire; perhaps cherished methods are crossed, and hallowed ideas overthrown, and this is not the smallest trial of good man's life. We almost think it needs a better man to make a good deacon than a good minister. *We* who preach the word go first, and this pleases human nature; grace is needed to make older, wealthier, and often wiser men go second and keep their place without envyings and bickerings; thousands do this, and are to be honoured for it.

We did not, however, take up our pen to eulogise deacons as a class, but simply to record our own happy experience, believing than one fact is better than a thousand theories. The deacons of our first village ministry were in our esteem the excellent of the earth, in whom, we took great delight. Hard-working men on the weekday, they spared no toil for their Lord on the Sabbath; we loved them sincerely, and do love them still, though another minister speaks of them with a severity never exceeded. In our idea they were as nearly the perfection of deacons of country church as the kingdom could afford, and we wonder that the present occupant of the pulpit could have found out faults and vices of which we never saw a trace.

Since our sojourn in London we have seen the burial of the fag-end of a race of deacons of whom only one survives, beloved and revered by all of us. A fine gentlemanly race, rather stuff and unmanageable, not quite to our mind, but honourable, respectable, prudent grandees of dissent the last generations of deacons were; men to be spoken of with reverence in all places where great memories are cherished. Our *own* growth of brethren are peculiarly lovable, active, energetic, warm-hearted generous men; but as we may have to live with them for another quarter of a century, we will only say of them that we could not exaggerate in speaking of our love to them as our generous-hearted follow soldiers and true yoke-fellows.

Of the one beloved father of the older school, who shares in all its excellences, and none of his grandiose stiffness, we give the best portrait that the best wood engraver in London could produce. Converted in early youth, Thomas Olney joined the church at Carter Lane in his youth, and for fifty-eight years he has remained in membership with the same people. For thirty years he has been a deacon. A dear lover of his departed pastor, Dr. [John] Rippon; he mourned his deceased very deeply, and thought that the glory was departed. He served the church under depressing changes of the pastorate, and then gave his heart to us without reserve, with very much of the juvenile ardour of a young man. He never acted as a drag to the wheels, or a dead weight to the chariot. His purpose was ready, and his heart and energy forced him with it to the front of the battle. In our great works of building the Tabernacle, the College, Orphanage, and Almshouses, he never lagged or so much as thought of holding back. Ten thousand blessings are upon him, and others of the same household, for the Lord's sake, and for the sake of the church of God. Flattery is far from us, but truth we must speak; we wish that every church had several honourable men. The poor among us call him blessed, and all of us hold him in our highest esteem.

We speak thus of men generally when they are dead; but it is a miserable policy which robs the living servant of Jesus of the little love-word which might have cheered declining years; it is more; it is an unworthy dishonesty which withholds the well-earned need of praise. Paul was not afraid to commend the living, nor need we be; and Paul never saw a warmer lover of the church of God than we see in our friend. May his last days be bright with dawn of heaven, and as his children and his children's children already walk in the truth, may he when gathered to his fathers amid their tears, be rejoiced over as a shock of corn fully ripe gathered into the garner. Meanwhile may he enjoy in his own heart an overflowing anticipation of the "Well done, good and faithful servant," which grace reserves for him.

3. Letter sent to the family of the late Thomas Olney, 1870 (*MB*)

ANNUAL CHURCH MEETING, February 2ⁿᵈ, 1870, Pastor C. H. Spurgeon presided.

Pastor J. A. Spurgeon read a letter which had been signed by the officers of the Church and sent to the family of the late [Thomas] Olney: Agreed that a copy be entered on the minutes.

"At a special Meeting of the Elders convened on [November] 28ᵗʰ, 1869 to consider the action to be taken by the officers of the Church upon the loss of our highly esteemed Senior Deacon and Elder Mr. Thomas

Olney, it was unanimously resolved, that the Pastors be requested to draw up a letter of condolence and sympathy to be afterwards forwarded to the bereaved family. Some delay has taken place in the carrying out of this which we are sure will not impute to any want of love or consideration upon the part of any of any of us. We now join to utter our sense of profound esteem for the high moral worth, the consistent Christian deportment, and the uniformly brotherly kindness, joined to ceaseless earnest activity, which at all times characterised our departed friend. We thankfully acknowledge the long continued and faithful services, which by the grace of God he was enabled to render to the church of which he was a member for 60 years. His memory will ever be cherished by us, as one of the 'excellent of the earth.' To his family, so many of whom we rejoice to see walking in communion with us, we desire to express our tenderest sympathy and earnest christian love, devoutly praying that the 'God of all consolation' may be pleased to sanctify to you and to one whole Church the loss which we have all sustained, in the departure of our Father Olney, from our fellowship, to the ranks of the glorified ones who are within the veil. Commending you all to his choicest blessings and comforts, whose consolations are rather few nor small.

We are, Dear Friends, Yours in the hope of everlasting life."

Signed by Elders and Deacons, C. H. Spurgeon and James H. Spurgeon, Pastors.

4. "Sketch of the Late Mr. Thomas Olney's Life," [1790-1869], January 1870* *(S&T)*

The Bible exhorts us to remember the way the Lord hath led us, and the fellow workers of our departed friend, Mr. [Thomas] Olney, earnestly desire to recall minding the loving care and tender mercy of God towards their esteemed and aged brother.

He was born November 10th, 1790, in Tring, in the country of Herts. His father, Mr. Daniel Olney, was for many years a deacon of the Baptist church in that town, Mr. Olney was sent to London from Tring, and apprenticed in the City to a wholesale mercer. He from his first entrance to London, attended the ministry of the well-known Dr. John Rippon, of the of Carter Lane Baptist Chapel. Here the Lord graciously met with him and saved his soul. He was proposed as a candidate for church fellowship, December 1809. If we take this for a starting point, then he was for 60 years a consistent and useful member of the church. In company with his brother, Mr. Daniel Olney, he was baptized and received into the church. Shortly after, he was married to Unity the daughter of Mr. Potter, deacon of the Baptist church, Amersham, Bucks. He was accustomed, even in their earliest years, to take his children to Carter Lane Chapel, having a little chair fixed on the pew seat for the youngest.

Here he formed friendships, faithful till death, with many old Baptist worthies. Between Dr. Rippon and our departed friend a most cordial friendship was formed. For many years he sat in the pulpit with him, and also assisted his weak and falling strength in administration of the ordinance of baptism.

The Sunday-school, the Baptist Home and Foreign Mission Societies, found in him a warm friend and liberal contributor.

In 1817, was commenced in Carter Lane Chapel an early Sabbath morning lecture. To be at the service by half-past six o'clock, to provide the necessary funds by collecting, to receive and welcome the various ministers, was to Mr. Olney at once a duty and delight. His closest and dearest friendships were formed within the circle of the church. Not only did he say of the church, "Thy God shall be my God," but also. "Thy people shall be my people."

Great changes took place in the church. In 1829, Carter Lane Chapel became the property of the City, and was pulled down; Dr. Rippon became old and feeble; the love of some grew cold, and they left the church in its hour of peril. Not so Thomas Olney: he remained manfully with the church. He was appointed a trustee for the chapel in New Park Street, opened in 1833. His much loved pastor and friend Dr. Rippon, expired in his presence, it might as properly be said in his arms. It was our honored friend's great privilege for some months by his care and kindness to cheer the last days of his highly esteemed friend and pastor, towards whose memory he cherished till his last days a most tender affection.

During all the time of erecting the new chapel in New Park Street, Mr. Olney may be said to have "favoured the very dust of Zion." From foundation to top stone he watched its progress with interest and prayer.

Prosperity was given under the ministry of Mr. James Smith, better known as Mr. Smith, of Cheltenham, the author of so many excellent little religious books. How gracious was God to our deceased brother? It was his happiness to see all his four sons baptized and join the church assembling within the walls of New Park Street Chapel. In 1838, he was, together his friend Mr. Winsor, chosen deacon of the church. He faithfully served that office thirty-one years. *He was ever remarkable for his early and constant attendance at the prayer-meeting, and other week-day services.* He truly loved the habitation of God's house but God had other mercies in store for him. His beloved Zion was to arise and shine. By the providence of God, Deacon Olney had his attention directed by his old friend, the late Mr. G. Gould, of Loughton, to our present honored pastor. The church was then seeking a minister, and from his recommendation Mr. C. H. Spurgeon was invited and became the honored and successful pastor of the church. Our Zion lengthened her chords and strengthened her stakes. The church abundantly grew and was multiplied.

A new and far larger building was needed, a meeting in Mr. Olney's house commenced the undertaking, and the work after much pains and prayer was accomplished. In 1855, "Father Olney", as he was playfully styled by pastor and deacon, was chosen treasurer of the church, and by the help of his sons fulfilled the office until his death, together with those of deacon and elder.

He was treasurer for fourteen years. "Of his love and devotion to both pastor and the church we all are witnesses." His greatest pride, we might almost use that word, was the work of God at the Tabernacle. He gloried and rejoiced in all that concerned the church. Every institution received his cordial co-operation; he loved college, orphanage, and almshouses, and helped them all to the extent of his ability. His fellow officers in the deaconship shared his esteem and love. And now that he has changed earthly for heavenly service and joy, may his memory and example stir us all to copy and follow him as far as he followed Christ.

Our departed friend had a childlike faith and humility. To believe in Jesus and to work for Christ was the very life of his new and better nature. He was eminently a true Baptist. In our departed "Father" the poor have lost a friend. The poor, and especially the poor of the church, always found in him sincere sympathy and help. By all his children his name will be in lasting remembrance and loving regard.

May the Lord raise others like him for his church's sake.

* It has pleased God to remove from us our most generous and indefatigable senior deacon of whom we gave our readers a portrait some months since. The loss to us is gain to him. Never minister had a better deacon; never church a better servant. We shall miss him in a hundred ways, and cannot but beseech the Lord to rise up others to fill the gaps, which he, and such as he are making, as one by one they leave us. The bibliographical notes here given are printed very nearly as we received them.

5. Testimonial Presented to William Olney and his reply, 1875 (*MB*)

1. Presentation of Testimonial to William Olney, (first elected in 1856), August 1875

To our Beloved Brother, William Olney, Senior Deacon of the Church, Worshipping at the Metropolitan Tabernacle:

Dear Friend:

We have all of us thanked God for many years for the gifts and graces with which He has seen fit to endow you, and for the spirit of love and burning zeal for which you have been distinguished. We are all sensible of the debt of gratitude which we owe to the Great Head of the Church for raising you up among us to be the friend and helper of us all from the Pastor to the youngest member. We all love you heartily and esteem you very highly for your works sake.

Therefore we have watched with deepest sorrow your declining health and severe afflictions and we have not ceased to pray for your complete restoration to health if the Lord will. We have groaned in spirit at the very thought of you being taken from us, and viewed your sickness as a chastisement upon us all. We have not failed to see that illness has by no means damped your ardour but has been sanctified to the maturing of your piety, and for this very reason we are the more solicitous that you may recover strength.

Dear brother your partial recovery has filled us all with hopeful joy, and we have made it the opportunity for presenting you with this token of our pure and fervent affection. You are very precious to us, for we see the spirit of your Master in you, and we long to have you among us for many years to come. Long may it be ere our Lord and Master shall say to you as he will do "well done, good and faithful servant." Peace be to you and your beloved household to which the Church has so many ties. May you live to a green old age as your honoured father did before you, and your beloved brothers, see the good of him all your days!

In the name of our Lord Jesus we wish you every blessing.

Signed on behalf of the whole Church at our meeting,

Pastors, Elders, Deacons, August 1875.

2. Reply to the Testimonial from William Olney, September 1875

Dear Pastors and dear Christian Friends:

I accept your very handsome present with great gratitude and warm and earnest thanks. It is all the more welcome to me coming as a testimonial of your Christian love and affection and not in any measure as a matter of merit and reward. In the latter sense it would have been incongruous and out of place as my 40 years connection with this Church has left me every year deeper and deeper in debt to the Church, in fact, under obligation which I shall never be able to repay. The day of my baptism and joining the Church was to me the happiest and best day of my life as here. I have found ever since then my choicest companions and dearest friends. In your worship and service I have spent the happiest hours of my life, here. I have learned the most important lessons which have been taught me from my youth up and in the service of this Church. I have found the noblest sphere of Christian work and have frequently been brought into such close fellowship with another world that heaven has began on earth and the soul has been filled with a joy unspeakable and full of glory. In giving myself to the Church at 15 years of age, I was enabled to do so fully and become at once from that time a regular attendant on the Sabbath and week day services which I have never ceased to attend regularly from that time until now. To this I owe very much of the joy and peace I have had in the service of the Lord and I feel confident there is no means of sanctification and growth in grace so effectual an earnest interest in the welfare of the Church to which you belong and a regular attendance at all its services. The week day services have very frequently been blest to my soul's good even more than those of the Sabbath day, and there is nothing I more strongly recommend to the younger membership of the Church than a regular attendance at the prayer meeting and week evening lectures. My first post of service for the Church was its Sabbath school and there I laboured for twenty years as Teacher, Secretary and Superintendent, afterwards in leading the singing at the week evening service and since then in the distribution of tracts, and visitation of the sick, in addressing the several bible classes, and in the office of Elder and Deacon.

It has been my privilege to secure the esteem of the five successive pastors who have presided over this Church during my membership though none of them have I been so indebted as to our present honoured and beloved pastor whose ministry has been to me as to many hundreds of thousands a constant source of instruction and joy.

I may say much more but I feel in the present state of my health it is not advisable. I will therefore conclude by again thanking you for the testimonial you have given me and by expressing the earnest prayer that this Church may continue to greatly prosper in every respect. Brethren, Peace be with you. Be steadfast, immovable always abounding in the work of the Lord.

William Olney

6. Officers of the Church at the Metropolitan Tabernacle, 1879

PASTORS: C. H. SPURGEON, J.A. SPURGEON
DEACONS: William Olney, William Higgs, Joseph Passmore, W. C. Murrell, T. R. Phillips, T. H. Olney, William Mills, W. Payne, B. W. Carr, T. Greenwood,
ELDERS: J. Ward, W. Perkins, G. Croker, W. Bowker, G. Court, H. White, R. Hellier, S. W. Longbotham, John T. Dunn, G. J. Marshall T. Davis, A. Nisbet, F. Cockrell, W. Gwillim, M Romang, W. Chilvers, S. R. Pearce, V. J. Charlesworth, J. Nicholson, J. Pullin, G. E. Elvin, G. Goldston. J Everett, C. Cornell, A. Wollard, M. Llewllyn, B. Corrick, W. H. Hale, E. Bingle.

The Pastor (C. H. Spurgeon) said: "It was a great blessing for a church that was increasing so numerously, that we were led to choose our brethren, the elders, who should watch over the church. Of all their gracious work in this church it is not within my power to tell. How much they do of holy service for God is written in the book above. I would again and again express my deep obligations both to my beloved deacons and the elders, for all that is done by them, and especially by those whom God honours by making them useful as the leaders of the church. Amongst us he that is the greatest does the most work, we know of no distinction but this: he is most honoured who is most the servant of all.

The elders do not always have pleasant duties; they see the dark side of the church when they lament over backsliding and falling into sin, and are forced to advise the church to exercise discipline. Yet how little of this has been required. If we had found one Judas in every twelve our exclusions would have been heart-breaking, but it has not been so. Doubtless there are tares among the wheat, but there have been few of those more manifest weeds which duty compels us to root up. I am sure that the elders will all heartily join in the utterance of thanksgiving by our elder Mr. Perkins, who is one of the oldest present" (*MV* 28).

Epilogue

While the Lord Jesus Christ was Spurgeon's "All in All", his motto for his church was "Go forward and never looked back." In 1878, the members of the Metropolitan Tabernacle looked forward to the twenty-fifth year of their union with their pastor. The church grew from 313 to 5,346 members. A testimonial was proposed, and a sum of "no less than £5000 as a thank-offering for the pastor was to be raised. £6,233 were raised and applied, at Spurgeon's insistence, with not a penny going to him, to various societies in the working church of the Metropolitan Tabernacle."

The main part of the Silver Anniversary of 1879 was Spurgeon's preaching of the two sermons on 18 May, 1879. "The Middle Passage" was preached in the morning and based on the text from Habakkuk 3:2—"O Lord, I have heard thy speech, and was afraid: O Lord, revive thy work in the midst of the years make known; in wrath remember mercy." It was Habakkuk's (as well as Spurgeon's) fear, prayer, and plea. He looked back, evaluated the present, and looked forward to the future. He stressed:

> We are in the middle passage, but if we have faith in God all is safe. We may go and leap in our duties over the mountains and the hills, and not be afraid that our foot will slip. We fall without our God, but with God

our feet shall never slide. He keepeth the feet of his saints, and when the wicked shall be silent in darkness then shall the strength of the Lord be seen (*MV* 14).

In the evening of the same day, Spurgeon preached on "The Crowning Blessings Ascribed to God", taking his text from Psalm 65:11: "Thou crownest the year with thy goodness". In his sermon, God's goodness was adored, confessed, and attributed to God alone. His plea to the members, the thousands present that evening, was to hold fast to the profession of Christ and to win souls for the Master. He said, "I care nothing about fine language, or about the pretty speculations of prophecy, or a hundred dainty things; but to break the heart and bind it, to lay hold on a sheep of Christ and bring it back to the fold, is the one thing I would live for" (*MV* 24).

On 19 May, 1879, two events were held to commemorate the silver anniversary: First, an afternoon tea for seven hundred of the "poor members of the church", followed by "a meeting for praise and thanksgiving". Two psalms were sung at the beginning: Psalm 103, "My souls, repeat his praise", and Psalm 89, "My never-ceasing songs will show". While the songs were sung and the people were coming in, Spurgeon said:

> We are to give up this time entirely to praise. We cannot divide prayer from praise, nor praise from prayer, for all supplication should be "with thanksgiving", and all thanksgiving is pretty sure to have prayer growing out of it. But this is to predominate tonight [see his "Address"], the praising and blessing of God for twenty-five years of mercy extended to us. It is little over the exact date, but that does not signify; we have a little more reason for thanksgiving on that account. Let us lift up our hearts with our voices, our souls with our songs, while we magnify our heavenly Father's name for all his loving-kindness (*MV* 27).

The second event was Spurgeon's "Address", and the theme of the address was gratitude and praise: "As we close this twenty-five years, we ascribe unto the glorious Jehovah all honour and praise for ever and ever . . . O give thanks unto the Lord, for he is good, and his mercy endureth for ever" (*MV* 38).

In the afternoon of Tuesday, 20 May, 1879, a tea was held for the contributors to the Bazaar and Testimonial Fund. In the evening, Mr. B. W. Carr and Rev. C. Stanford presented their papers (see Part II of this publication) followed by the testimonial meeting and the presentation of the testimonial by William Olney. Charles Spurgeon made the final comments for the day that included a request and a testimony:

> *I beg you to pray very much for me that I may be held up for years to come. I shall be, by the Lord's grace. We stand on a rock which does not move. We have a gospel to preach which is not exhausted, and we trust in a Spirit who never deserts those who confide in him. We are not afraid for the future, but, brethren pray for us more ever, for your prayers are our riches* (*MV* 75).

Endnotes

1   There are sixty-three volumes to the Metropolitan Tabernacle Pulpit Series. Readers interested in Spurgeon and sermon literature may consult and read the following compiled by Dr. Terence Peter Crosby: *C. H. Surgeon's Sermons Beyond Volume 63*, (2009); *C. H. Spurgeon's Early Sermons*, (2010); *C. H. Spurgeon's Forgotten Prayer Meeting Addresses,* (2011). All three are published by Day One Publications, Leominster, UK. On sermon literature, consult: Keith A. Francis and William Gibson, *The Oxford Handbook of the British Sermon 1689–1901*, (Oxford 2012).

2   The following sources (perused at the Evangelical Library, London) contain short accounts of the Metropolitan Tabernacle as the working church and Spurgeon's Silver Anniversary: Geo. C. Needham, *Life and Labours of Charles H. Spurgeon,* (Boston, 1883), 143–46. Needham lists twenty-six societies (i.e., associations/ institutions) in the church; G. Holden Pike, *The Life and Work of Charles Haddon Spurgeon, Volume VI,* (London, 1894), 229–32; Rev. R. Shindler, *From the Usher's Desk to the Tabernacle Pulpit: The Life and Labours of Pastor C. H. Spurgeon*. Authorized Edition, (London, 1897), see Chapter XI, "The Metropolitan Tabernacle", 109–128; G. Barnett Smith, *Spurgeon: The People's Preacher,* (London, n.d), 217–22; George J. Stevenson, *Pastor C. H. Spurgeon: His Life and Work to His Forty-Third Birthday* (London, 1877), 94–108.

3   See: Iain M. Murray, *The Forgotten Spurgeon*, (1966); Lewis Drummond, *Spurgeon: Prince of Preachers*, (1992); Ernest W. Bacon, *Spurgeon: Heir of the Puritans*, (1967); Peter Morden, *C. H. Spurgeon, The People's Preacher*, (2009); Peter Morden, *"Communion with Christ": The Spirituality of C. H. Spurgeon*, (2010); Tom Nettles, *Living By Revealed Truth: The Life and Pastoral Theology of Charles Haddon Spurgeon*, (2013).

4   From bookmarks printed by Pilgrim Publications, n.d.

5   This writer used the pristine copy of the *Memorial Volume* in the *Minute Books* at the Metropolitan Tabernacle in 2012 and 2013 and a copy of the *Memorial Volume: Spurgeon's Silver Wedding Testimonial Services*, at the Evangelical Library (Special Collections) in 2013. Spurgeon wrote an article on "Twenty-five Years ago", a fragment in *The Sword and the Trowel* (January 1879). In his Autobiography (Volume IV, Chapter LXXXIV), twelve pages were devoted to the twenty-fifth anniversary held in 1879: "A Double Silver Wedding", 15–26. The latter is omitted from this documentary history to avoid repetition of the historical account of the Silver Anniversary of the Metropolitan Tabernacle. Also, see C. H. Spurgeon, *The Metropolitan Tabernacle: Its History and Work*, (Reprinted by Pilgrim Publications, 1990) and *Memorial Volume. Mr. Spurgeon's Jubilee: Report on the Proceedings at the Metropolitan Tabernacle, on Wednesday and Thursday Evenings, 18–19 June, 1884,* (London: Passmore & Alabaster, 1884).

6   Hereinafter, the abbreviations *MB (*for *Minute Books)*, *MV (*for *Memorial Volume)*, and *S&T (*for *The Sword and the Trowel)* will be used especially for Parts I and II of this documentary history, and the appendices.

7   An interested reader may peruse these letters in *The Suffering Letters of C. H. Spurgeon* (Annotations by Hannah Wyncoll, Wakeman Trust, 2007). One can garner many valuable insights from *The Suffering Letters*. Spurgeon said, "maintain the prayer meetings at blood-heat. See well to the schools and all the classes, and other labours for Jesus Christ. Let nothing flag of prayer, service, or offering. We have a great trust, may the Lord make us faithful". (Written from Cannes, January 31 [probably 1878], 23–4), and from the *Minute Books:* "We must go from strength to strength, and be a missionary church, and never rest until not only this neighbourhood, but our country . . . shall be enlightened with the gospel." (1854). The *Minute Books* also reveal an irritation of the pastor. On 5 March, 1866, Spurgeon certified the minutes of the church meeting held after the prayer meeting and found the writing pens highly unsatisfactory. He wrote in the minutes, "Shocking pens, it being a custom to use the worst possible pens in our vestry." Better pens were supplied to the pastor after this meeting.

8   John Flavel, *The Mystery of Providence* (The Banner of Truth Trust, 1678, 1963, reprinted 2002).

9   Reading the *Minute Books (MB)* yielded additional insights on Spurgeon. His loved his Master, and his flock was a dominant theme. Undoubtedly, his work as a preacher proved to be very stressful on many occasions. Indeed, Spurgeon was a "bruised reed" that His Master loved to lift up.

10 See his book, *The Dominance of Evangelicalism: the Age of Spurgeon and Moody*, (InterVarsity Press, Downers Grove, 2005). Dr. Crosby is also the compiler of the six-volume set of *365 days with Spurgeon*.

11 I assume sole responsibility for any shortcomings in this documentary history. The original (British) spelling has been maintained. Paragraphs in the addresses have been divided and shortened, and some punctuation marks have been edited. Antiquated expressions remain the same as found in the addresses, prayers, and selections.